The Expat Guide to Living in Bali

MICHAEL HENRY

Copyright © 2014 Michael Henry

All rights reserved.

ISBN-13: 978-1497550919

DEDICATION

This book is dedicated to my loving wife and son.

CONTENTS

Disclaimer

1	Introduction	Pg 1
2	Moving to Bali Checklist	Pg 10
3	Settling In	Pg 13
4	What to Bring to Bali	Pg 16
5	Where to Live in Bali	Pg 21
6	Renting a House	Pg 23
7	Education	Pg 28
8	Health	Pg 56
9	Cost of Living	Pg 62
10	Finding Work	Pg 66
11	Managing Staff	Pg 68
12	General and Useful Information	Pg 73
13	Getting the Right Visa	Pg 83
14	Scams and Warnings	Pg 88
15	Things to do in Bali	Pg 92
16	Bali Business Guide	Pg 95
17	Internet Resources	Pg 98
18	Expat Interview	Pg 101
19	Final Thoughts	Pg 107

DISCLAIMER

All external links to external parties in this guide are for information purposes only. They are provided as a courtesy and inclusion does not imply endorsement by BaliExpat.com.

This document is a publication of BaliExpat.com Copyright 2014 BaliExpat.com. All rights reserved worldwide. No portion of this document in part or whole, can be used without the express written consent of the author.

This material is for informational purposes only. All material contained in this guide is provided in good faith and accurate as possible. No liability will be accepted for any errors or omissions, or any loss or damages incurred in using this guide.

Prices, laws and economic conditions are subject to change. Readers should check with the relevant authorities as individual situations will vary. Financial, visa, insurance and tax matters should be checked with relevant authorities and qualified persons before making any personal arrangements.

1 INTRODUCTION

Climb aboard for the biggest adventure of your life! If you are reading this, you must have decided, or are at least thinking about moving to Bali. You might even be already living in Bali and you are now finding your way around this island paradise. Once you leave the confines of a hotel and venture out of the tourist areas, Bali can sometimes be a bit of a shock to the system. I wrote this book to help ease your transition into your new life on Bali.

Who Is this Book For?

While you can find plenty of travel information on Bali and various information for retirees moving to Bali, since starting a family myself, I found there is not a great deal available for families moving or living in Bali. Moving abroad to any country as a family, is a huge challenge. Bali presents even more challenges, and this book will hopefully help you to prepare for the move, settle in and help to explain some of the common problems you may encounter along the way and how to deal with them. If you are still on the fence about the move, this book will give you a good idea of what to expect, as it doesn't take long for anyone to realize that living in Bali is not all about sitting around a pool, sipping cocktails.

As the world becomes more global, the whole definition of 'work' and a 'work place' has changed. International relocation for work, has become more common. The internet has enabled more people to become 'location independent' where they no longer have to commute to an office, but can work anywhere in the world they choose. Some people work in very remote locations on oil rigs and mines, while their families live in another place. They are referred to as: fly in, fly out workers (FIFO). These changes have enabled some families to choose where they want to live in the world, rather than just living in the same place they were born.

Bali has become a popular choice for many families, as evidenced by the growing number of international schools on the island. Bali is just one island that makes up the archipelago of Indonesia. Indonesia is a developing country, with the fourth largest population in the world, spanning across more than 900 inhabited islands. Spurned on by tourism, Bali is experiencing rapid growth and its already sagging infrastructure, cannot keep up. Bali has a fascinating, but complex culture, which can also at times be a source of frustration for expats. So while there are many things to love about living in Bali, there are many new problems you will face along the way.

Why Bali?

I run a couple of different websites about living in Bali, and everyday I receive emails from people with various questions about moving to Bali. Living in Bali has also become something of a hot topic in the Australian media, with frequent stories about Australian families living in Bali. Many of the stories focus on fly-in, fly-out workers (FIFO). These workers typically work on mines in Australia, or offshore oil rigs and work for two weeks straight and then have two weeks holiday.

With the boom in mining, inflation has skyrocketed in Australia; so while families might make good money working on the mines, the price of living has increased proportionately. This has led to families seeking places to live outside of Australia, and sometimes other previously popular expat hot spots, such as Hong Kong and Singapore. Bali is increasingly on the radar for these families. The cost of living is low and living on the island has a permanent holiday vibe.

This trend has pushed property prices up in Bali, but rental prices are still cheaper than most Australian cities. Food and gasoline prices are considerably cheaper than most western countries. In fact, gasoline is actually subsidized by the government and is a fraction of people pay in western countries. This is likely to change at some point in the future as it is not economically sustainable for the government.

Even though many of these articles in the media cite a low cost of living for families wanting to live in Bali, I believe that anyone who moves to Bali purely for economic reasons, could be making a huge mistake. I would also like to point out, that even though there is a great deal of coverage, at least in the Australian media given to fly-in, fly-out workers, they are just one of the profiles of families moving to Bali. There are a wide range of backgrounds and nationalities of families living in Bali. So other than cost of living, what are some of the other reasons why you might want to live in Bali?

Raising kids in Bali

If you have ever traveled with your kids to Bali, it does not take long to realize that Balinese and Indonesians in general, adore children. There is a saying in Indonesian: 'Banyak anak, banyak rezeki'. Banyak means many. Anak, child or children and rezeki means support or sustenance. The belief if that your children will help to take care of you, when you are too old to continue working. This is quite common in Asian culture where there are no retirement funds or pensions.

Before we had our son, everyone would always ask when were going to have kids. Then as soon as we had our son, people asked when were going to have another one!

Walk into a hotel and the staff will start smiling and waving at your kids. If you have a young child, the staff at a hotel or restaurant, will often pick up your kids and take them around. It might be a shock for some parents new to Bali, but I know have gotten used to it. Everywhere you go people will ask your child's name, how old they are etc. etc. It was actually a bit strange for me when I went back to Australia for a short holiday, when no-one except for family, did this.

Balinese are very proud of their own children, so you will often get into a conversation about peoples' families with everyone you meet. While some couples might make a decision not to have children, this is pretty much unheard of in Bali.

There is an old proverb: "It takes a village to raise a child." This could easily apply to how children are raised in Bali. Families all tend to live together in a compound, with generations of a family all living together. Neighbors' kids will all play together and it is hard sometimes trying to figure out whose child belongs to who.

While Balinese adore kids, you may also wonder at other times if this really true when you see whole families riding together on a motorcycle, without any helmets. So yes, personal safety is different in Bali, something which I will discuss later in the book.

I haven't raised kids in my own country, so I can only get an idea of what it is like from my own friends and family and what I see in the media. I see many families that have both parents working and their kids are put in child care, if they are not going to school. In the US it is standard to have metal detectors in schools and I saw a report on CNN where a company is launching a new product - bullet proof armor, to be put into kids school back packs.

Parents are stressed out working, commuting and bringing kids back and forth from work to day care. Kids typically spend most of their time indoors playing computer games. Child obesity is a growing problem, along with a long list of disorders like ADHD (attention deficit disorder).

Most families in Bali are not well off to say the least and some live in extreme poverty. The kids always seems happy though—content playing outside with just an old soccer ball, throwing rocks or flying kites.

If you send your children to an international school, they will more than likely be studying with kids from around the world. I can think of no better geography or sociology lesson than living abroad in a different culture. There is also the opportunity to learn an additional language, which has a huge range of cognitive and social benefits. I have seen local kids playing with foreign kids who are here on holidays and it is amazing how quickly start playing together even though they cannot speak each others languages.

Affordable home help

Up until we had our first child, we didn't employ a maid or any staff. When we first moved to Bali, we lived in a small house which was pretty easy to clean and maintain. I thought it was pretty strange how all of the expats I knew, employed a team of staff including cooks, maids, gardeners, drivers etc. It seemed like more effort managing the staff than just doing things yourself. My wife and I enjoyed our privacy also and couldn't imagine having someone else in our house all of the time.

Since we started a business, we have become more comfortable employing staff. Then after my wife gave birth to our son, I suggested we get a maid or *pembantu* for a few months to help my wife. Now I couldn't imagine life without Ketut, our *pembantu*. She is a great worker and a nice person to have around the house. Our son adores her also. Before we employed a maid, I also wondered how some families became so attached to their *pembantu*. Now I can see why, and it is easy to start feeling your staff as part of your family.

Salaries are quite low in Indonesia and good jobs are not easy to come by, so not only is it great having staff to take care of all of the chores in your house, it is a good feeling to be providing much needed employment. I will discussing this in more detail later in the book, but it is certainly one of the great benefits of living in Bali.

One word of warning however, don't let yet your kids to become lazy and relying on your *pembantu* to take over their household chores.

Schools

Most expats send their children to international schools. As the foreign population has increased in Bali, so have the schooling options. There are a range of educational programs available including Monterrosi and the International Baccalaureate (IB) program. Going to an international school will give your children exposure to a range of cultures, and they will have the ability to meet other kids from around the world.

Weather

Bali lies just 8 degrees south of the equator, ensuring year round warm weather. Bali has just two seasons: dry and rainy. Even in rainy season, the showers typically don't last too long. If you and your family enjoy an outdoor lifestyle, you will love living in Bali. The weather is conducive to a range of outdoor activities and sports. I have yet to find any kids that don't love swimming and the biggest problem is actually getting them out of the pool.

Activities

Bali has a wide range of activities and things to do for kids and teenagers. There is so much to do and many of the activities are relatively inexpensive. I don't think it is possible to ever feel bored living in Bali. Bali is a compact island, yet the different areas around Bali vary quite dramatically, so it is convenient and inexpensive to travel around on weekends. Java, Lombok and the Gilli Islands are also easy to get to for a short or extended trip.

Is Bali right for you and your family?

This is the part of the book where I try to convince you not to move to Bali. Why would I do this? Bali is not going be for everyone. I feel that it is a good idea to be up front about the problems Bali is currently experiencing, so you can decide now if they are going to be a deal breaker for you. It is certainly going to save you a lot of trouble, not to mention the expense of moving, if you are at least familiar with some of the typical problems expats face moving to Bali.

Corruption

Not a days seems to go by without a story of corruption in the news. Corruption is endemic in Indonesia from the highest levels of government, down to the very bottom. There is some attempt being made to clamp down, but even if someone is caught and sentenced to prison, the system is so corrupt that the offenders may not even spend a single day in jail. It can be quite depressing as in the long run it affects the future development of the country.

Expats living in Bali will typically only face corruption when driving on the roads or applying for a visa. If you are running a business based in Bali or working, you might have to deal with it more. Police often target foreigners for real or imagined driving infractions. The important thing is to carry a valid driver's license, your vehicle registration and to wear a helmet if you are riding a motorbike, and you shouldn't have any problems with the police.

If you do have to pay a fine, you can choose to pay on an on the spot cash fine or get a ticket and have to make a court appearance. Most people choose the first option and negotiate to pay anywhere from 50,000 to 200,000 rupiah for minor infractions, like doing an illegal turn. The cash fine will go straight into the policeman's pocket. It could feel a little strange the first time as in most countries bribing a police officer is a serious crime. Not that I recommend it, but some foreigners (and locals) don't even bother to get a driver's license and if they ever get pulled over, just pay the fine. Of course if you have an accident and don't have a license, it will only lead to more problems.

The other place you will face corruption, is when you apply for a visa. When you get any kind of visa in Indonesia, basically you have two options. Do it all yourself, which can mean several trips to the immigration office, being made to wait for long periods at the immigration office and in general an endless source of frustration, especially if you are new to Indonesian bureaucracy. The alternative is to use an agent, who will do all of this on your behalf and pay extra fees to expedite your application.

So while corruption is rife in Indonesia, it should not affect your day to day life. You can be sure however, if you get together with a few expats, everyone will have plenty of stories to tell about corruption.

Traffic

Traffic jams are an increasing problem in Bali. A trip that should take 20 minutes, can take more than three hours during peak traffic times and can even be worse if something is blocking traffic, like an accident. Motorbikes are the preferred choice of transport for Balinese, and it is common to see people reading motorbikes on side walks and driving down the wrong side of a street. As wealth increases more people are buying cars and then add in the many trucks and tourist buses ploughing the island and it doesn't take long to realize the problems of getting around.

One of the worst bottle necks is the Simpang Siur roundabout. A series of 'underpasses' have been built to help ease the congestion. The problem is that more and more new cars are added to the roads each day. The only solution, if you can call it that, is to try and live close to your child's school or your place of work.

Rubbish

For anyone who loves Bali, it is very sad to see the growing piles of trash all over the island. Rubbish is thrown into rivers, which only flows out to the sea and then back onto the beaches. It is estimated that around three quarters of the rubbish in Bali is not collected at all. It is left to rot or burnt—including the plastic waste, releasing dangerous toxins into the air. There is almost no comprehension in Indonesia, of the dangers of breathing in this toxic air. There is some effort being made to recycle at least some of the waste, but it is almost impossible to keep up with the waste, especially the plastic.

Water/electric

There are basically no dams on Bali. Some of the water comes from natural lakes, but most of the water is pumped from under the ground. This supply however is already drying up and as the water table rises, salinity is becoming a problem. Since there is no sewerage system, septic tanks are sometimes built right alongside water wells. Installing tanks and taking advantage of rain catchments is one solution in high rainfall areas.

With the growth in tourism and population in Bali, the demand for electricity is also increasing at a rapid rate. Black outs are not too uncommon and when we first moved to Bali, the PLN (the national electric company) was doing maintenance on their power stations and there were scheduled power outages once a week. It is of course inconvenient having no power, but it was kind of fun using candles and being without electronic devices for a while. It also makes you appreciate electricity so much more. Bali is actually well serviced by power compared with many other islands in Indonesia, some of which can only get it a few hours per day.

Crime

Bali is generally a very safe place to live. The government, local community and police understand the importance of the link between tourism and crime. The strong sense of community in Bali offers some protection, but with the influx of workers coming from other islands to work, it is almost inevitable that some will turn to crime in order to survive. Home burglaries are the most common, along with bag snatching from motorbikes.

Gangs often target villas and homes of foreigners, looking for cash and other valuables, like mobile phones and laptop computers. It is important to assess your home for potential security problems. Villas located in isolated places are particularly vulnerable. Keeping dogs and hiring a security guard are just a couple of ways to minimize risk.

Slow internet

One of the biggest sources of frustrations for many foreigners moving to Bali, is slow internet. According to speedtest.net, Indonesia ranks 122 in the world for internet speed. The more remote your residence, the less options you have for reliable internet. If you depend on fast internet for your work or business, you could have problems living in Bali.

Health

The standard of health care in Bali is not as high as what you are probably used to. Doctors and hospitals can handle general ailments, but for serious health issues or major operations, you will need to travel to Singapore or Australia for medical care. Therefore, it is imperative that your insurance covers medical evacuations.

Education

While there are many well known schools in Bali, the standard of education is not as high as in most western countries. The schools employ foreign and western educated teachers, but the facilities are generally not as good as what you might find in your home country. There is sometimes a high turn over of staff as teachers are often on one year contracts. Many families also only stay in Bali for one year, possibly making it difficult for your children if you plan to stay long term. While there are many things to do in Bali, there are generally less sporting and organized clubs than what you might find in your home country.

2 MOVING TO BALI CHECK LIST

Once you have decided on a moving date, it is a good idea to start a 'to do' list for everything that needs to be completed before you step onto that plane.

Here are just some things that you might need to put on your list:

Three months before the move:

- Check that your passports are valid for at least 12 months, or 18 months, if you are applying for a KITAS.

- Make sure you have internet banking set up with your bank account in your home country. This can be useful for sending money to Bali or for paying any bills in your home country, while you are away.

- Start getting some quotes for shipping your household goods

- Organize health insurance for your family. Check the policy carefully to see you are well covered in Bali, and make sure the policy includes emergency evacuation.

- If you are applying for a KITAS before leaving for Bali, make sure you start the process well in advance.

- Visit a doctor that specializes in travel medicine to get advice on necessary injections and inoculations for your family.

- Start making contact with real estate agents in Bali.

- If you are renting out your house in your home country while you are away, start making arrangements with real estate agents and property managers

- Book your plane tickets to Bali

- Contact your child's school and notify them of your plans

Four weeks to go

- Start organizing clothes that you want to take to Bali. Possibly give away any old clothes to charity if you no longer need them.

- If you are applying for a social or sosbud visa, apply now

- Photocopy all of your travel and important documents. Consider also scanning and uploading them to an internet service like Dropbox.

- Arrange a place to store the belongings you won't be bringing to Bali

- Take the opportunity to have a clean out and sell or give away items that you no longer need.

- Cancel any automatic online payments, like gym memberships

- If you take any medications, make sure you have adequate supply

- It is too expensive to ship cars to Bali, so consider selling it

- Return any library books

- Get an international driver's license

- Get your finances in order before you leave - credit cards, mortgage payments etc.

Last Week

- Close utility accounts for your telephone, electricity, gas etc.

- Pack boxes and bags that you will be bringing with you. Include the items that you know you
   will need in the first few weeks such as your child's toys and books.

- Change your address at any companies that you will continue using their service, like banks and insurance.

3 SETTLING IN AND DEALING WITH CULTURE SHOCK

Moving to Bali is an exciting but stressful time for you and your family. You will be losing the familiarity of your home environment and the support network of your family and friends. With a little effort, however, you will start making new friends fairly quickly. In a small number of cases, the stress of moving can be a very serious problem. Pre-existing physical and mental health issues can easily be exacerbated by the move.

There is said to be four phases of culture shock. Firstly, there is the so called honeymoon period. This is when you still feel like you are on an extended vacation. Perhaps you are staying in a hotel until you find more permanent accommodation. Everything is new and exciting and everyone seems so friendly and helpful.

The next stage is a period of anger or frustration at living in your new surroundings, and is likely to be triggered by some kind of unpleasant experience. Maybe you had something stolen or you had trouble communicating. You may also go through periods of homesickness when you miss people or things from your home country. It is a difficult period to get through, and you may even think about going back 'home'.

Once you get through these stages, life will start to take on a degree of normality. You start developing a routine and you become more familiar with Balinese ways and the culture. The fourth stage is when you become a master of living in Bali— fluent in the language and at ease with the local culture.

Culture Shock and Children

Children tend to be more resilient and adapt quicker to new situations than adults. They can however, be affected by moving countries in different ways. It is difficult for children to comprehend distance and time for example and they may think that they can meet up with their old friends at any time.

When you have decided to move to Bali, start preparing them early for the move. Llana from Proed.asia suggests hanging up a calendar on the wall and counting down the days to the move. She also suggests to incorporate the move into story telling and using visual aids to help give your kids more of an idea of what to expect. It is also important to discuss the different culture, food and currency that they will be using.

Local children may run up and touch your kids, which might make them feel uncomfortable. In western countries there is a fairly defined feeling of personal space, but not so in Indonesia. It could take your children some time getting used to, but they also might even enjoy being the center of attention.

After making the move, talk to your children as much as possible and be honest. Don't for example, say you are going 'home' soon, if you are not. Keep in touch with family and friends via Skype. Make sure to have some of your child's favorite food with you, as it might take some time for them to get used to the different food in Bali.

Be mindful of your own stress and frustration of moving, as children pick up on this very easily. Try to establish a routine as quickly as possible, with set meal and bed times.

Reverse culture shock

Most people are aware of the phenomena of culture shock when traveling to a different country, but what is less well known is reverse culture shock, which some people experience when they return to their home country after spending time abroad.

You will look at your country with a different set of eyes. Some things will make you happy, like being able to buy all of your favorite foods again, but other things might take time to get used to again.

Living in Bali is very laid back, something which doesn't take long to get used to for many expats. Going back to a fast paced, western lifestyle may take some time getting used to again. You will also get used to the strong community life Bali has and it might be a shock when you go back to see people in your neighborhood mostly ignoring each other.

Moving back will also be difficult for your children. They might get singled out and treated differently by their peers. You might consider sending your kids to an international school in your home country, or a school which has students from a variety of cultural backgrounds.

4 WHAT TO BRING TO BALI AND WHAT TO LEAVE BEHIND

It is amazing how our 'stuff' accumulates over time without even realizing it. It is only really when you move house and you have to calculate how big of a truck or shipping container, you need to move everything, do you realize how much you have. Before I got married I was constantly traveling and moving house. "Don't let your possessions own you", became my mantra. It is a good way to live your life. Now that I have a family, I do understand how it is easy to become sentimentally attached to certain things.

If you have things kept in closets that you have not touched for more than six months, you probably have to question whether you still need them. I know some people who shipped everything they owned to Bali and later regretted it. Shipping is a huge expense. Even if you can afford to send everything, it is still a huge hassle and potential source of stress. Things can get damaged or lost in the move; you might find that many of the things in your 'old' life have no use in Bali. Houses in Bali also don't tend to have have much storage space. You might want to take the opportunity to relieve yourself of some of your possessions by selling or giving them away.

Once you have decided to move to Bali, you might want to start labeling things in your house: take, sell or give away. This will help give you time to decide if the things you label 'take', you will actually need in

Bali.

Which shipping option you decide on will depend on how much stuff you have. If money is not a problem, or your company is paying for your moving costs, you will probably want to use a full service, door-to-door shipping company. There are several international relocation companies available such as Crown Relocation or Allied. These companies will handle all aspects of moving your goods, like dealing with customs. The downside is that they are not cheap.

All containers shipped to Bali, enter Indonesia through the port of Surabaya. Technically if you have a KITAS you are allowed to import personal belongings free of charge. This being Indonesia you might be asked to pay some duty for your goods to clear customs.

When researching shipping companies and getting quotes, you should check exactly what it includes and what extra charges are not included, such as: terminal handling, port service, container stuffing, pickup and delivery to wharf, export customs clearance, documentation, handling, bill of lading fees or any other export charges. On the Indonesian side you need to check: import charges, customs clearance and delivery.

If you have just a few boxes to send, you might want to consider sending them air mail through your regular post office. You will obviously need an address to send them to. If you are starting a job in Bali, perhaps your company can help you out. I have a friend who moved to Bali from the US recently and she sent a number of boxes by mail. They all arrived safely and there was no extra customs fees to pay. I have read many complaints about stuff not arriving by post in and out of Bali, but personally I have never had trouble. You can also the services of international delivery companies like DHS or UPS, but they are more expensive. The one time I had a book delivered to me by UPS, I had to pay about the same price of the book in duty.

What to bring

These days it is getting easier to find almost everything you need in Bali. It can sometimes be frustrating trying to track things down, but that can also be part of the fun of moving, and you might even discover new stores along the way.

"Food is something we miss a lot from home, we regularly ask friends visiting to bring things for us. Haircare products is another thing we bring (waxes, hairspray etc not shampoo). Also while you can get them things like cards, wrapping paper etc I bring from home as you can't just go to the shop and get them easily as I found out the first time I needed kids birthday cards on the party day!"

Medication

If you require any medication, you should consult with your doctor and buy enough medicine to last you until you can find a similar or alternative drug in Bali. You can also try emailing one of the international hospitals in Bali and check if your medicine is available. In general, you do not require a prescription to buy drugs in Bali. If it is not available in Bali and have to buy it in Singapore for example, you will need a prescription.

Patricia from Singapore gives the following advice:

"One piece of advice I can give is to know your entire family's health history. If possible, have it written down for each family member, especially if you need specific medication. Find out whether they can be obtained at the pharmacy in Bali. If not, how do you plan to get supplies in the time that you are in Bali? Would you consider holistic therapies (acupuncture, reiki, essential oils etc) for your conditions? If yes, be prepared for a huge lifestyle change in terms of diet, life and how you view life. Another would be to be open to change. You will not have a lot of the food, personal care, and luxury items that you are used to when living at home. Rather than lament this, why not take it as an opportunity to try a different way of living? Simplify, go back to basics, and appreciate what you have, rather than lament about what you lack. Here's a biggie: the Balinese culture is extremely different from your home culture, even if you are an Asian moving here from an Asian country. I'm a good example - Singaporean Chinese moving to Bali. The Balinese lifestyle, way of dealing with people and situations, approach to religion and work, are all vastly different from what you know. So be prepared for some cultural differences."

Clothing

If you are tall or a larger person, you could have difficulty finding shoes and clothes that fit comfortably in Bali. There are however, quite a few boutiques catering to foreigners and you can also get just about anything made up by a tailor in Bali, for a reasonable cost. Stocking up on underwear can be a good idea for both men and women.

Ebook Reader

I love reading and I always had difficulty find reading material in Bali, until I bought myself a Kindle. Kindles are not available in Indonesia, so I would suggest getting a Kindle or some other kind of electronic reader.

Kitchen Utensils

I have found all of the kitchen utensils here that I need. Ace Hardware has a great range, but no potato mashers!

Coffee Maker

Coffee machines like Delonghi and Saeco can be found in Bali, but they are very expensive. On my last trip back to Australia I bought a Delonghi machine. I checked the price at online store in Indonesia and it was double what I paid. Netspresso type machines are not available here, so you might want to avoid bringing one of those machines, unless someone can send you the capsules.

Sense of Humor

Perhaps one of the most important things you will need in Bali!

What to leave behind

It sometimes makes me wonder why people want to ship their furniture halfway around the world. Due to the weight and size, it is rather impractical to ship. You can find great furniture in Bali that is relatively inexpensive and is more than likely more suitable to the climate.

Electrical goods like televisions, washing machines and fridges are also something you should leave at home. Other than that they are expensive to ship, most houses in Bali don't have high wattage, making some high energy appliances unusable. Anything that requires a high amount of energy to start, like a water kettle, might have trouble. Indonesia uses 220V with two pin plugs, and you can buy various adapters for things like mobile phone chargers and laptop computers, which generally don't have a problem.

> *"About 7 years ago, I had some friends bring me a Kambrook electric wok. It can only be used as a golf fish bowl."*

I think for furniture and household electrical goods, you are better off selling or giving away what you currently own, and then buying everything new when you get to Bali. When you move back home, as long as everything is kept in reasonable condition, you won't have trouble selling them again in Bali. You could also give them away to local friends or to charities, who will happily accept any donations.

If you are planning on bringing bed sheets to Bali, you need to be aware that bed sizes are different in Indonesia to most parts of the world.

Cars and motorbikes are expensive to ship, together with the duties you will be required to pay, cost prohibitive.

> *"I know of someone that owns and runs a hotel here, that imported an old motorbike from England. Bike got to Surabaya and customs wanted 30 million rupiah. Friend then said no-way, sent bike back to Singapore where he had it taken completely apart and sent back as spares. Customs laughed and said there would be 100 per cent import duty on antique spares. Friend then had to re-export the pieces of his bike back to the UK."*

5 WHERE TO LIVE IN BALI

Before you begin to look at any houses, it is a good idea to decide on an area that you would like to live. All of the different areas in Bali where expats live, have their own kind of vibe, along with various pluses and minuses. With the traffic problems in Bali, it can be a good idea to choose your schools first and then base your decision on where to live from that.

The main areas in the south of Bali include: Seminyak, Kuta, Canggu, Sanur, Renon, Denpasar, Jimbaran and Nusa Dua. Along the east coast you have Candidasa, Padang Bai and Amed. Along the north coast is Singaraja and Lovina. In central Bali you have Ubud and the many villages surrounding it.

Seminyak

Seminyak is popular with expats, mainly for its beach, restaurants and nightlife. It is generally the 'go to' place for the young and beautiful. Its popularity reflects the property prices and property owners tend to target short term tourists, where they can make the most money.

Canggu

Canggu has also become a popular area for expats. The rice fields are sadly being taken over by more villas, so don't expect that beautiful rice field view to last for long. Canggu is home to Bali's only expat club, the Canggu Club. The Canggu Club offers a range of sporting and recreational facilities, a restaurant and bar. Right next door to the

Canggu Club is the Canggu Community School (www.ccsbali.com). Umalas sits between Seminyak and Canggu and it is also popular with expats.

Kerobokan

Kerobokan is located north-east of Seminyak and is perhaps most famous for the notorious 'Kerobokan Jail'. Since it is further away from the beach, property prices are a little less than Seminyak. The Australia International School is located in Kerobokan.

Sanur

Located on the eastern side of south Bali, Sanur has a reputation for being popular with retired expats. It is a little less crazy than the Kuta/Seminyak area, making it popular also for young families. Sanur has a 5km jogging/cycle path along the beach, which is great for getting some exercise. The beaches are calm and are good for swimming, wind surfing and kite surfing. Sanur has many of Bali's international schools, including Bali International School, Djatmika International School and Sanur Independent School. It also has several well known pre-schools such as 'Cheeky Monkeys'.

Ubud

Ubud is often regarded as the 'cultural center' of Bali, it is also fast becoming the center for yoga and all things organic. It is popular with expats looking for a quiet place to live and to have more of cultural experience in Bali. Many families attending Green School live in Ubud, even though it is a little out of town. Pelangi School is also located in Ubud.

Lovina

Lovina is a small town located on the north coast of Bali. It is much quieter than the other areas listed here and property prices are much more reasonable. There is also a newly opened National Plus school in Lovina: www.northbalibilingualschool.org

6 RENTING A HOUSE

Finding a suitable house or villa to live is going to be your first big challenge moving to Bali. Renting a property in Bali is quite different from probably what you are used to. While there are real estate agents, you can also find suitable properties through word of mouth, classified ads, on the web, or simply by driving around the area you want to live in and looking out for 'For Rent' signs.

It is important not to rush into something too quickly. A good idea is to first stay in a hotel for a few days or weeks and spend your time looking for a property. Don't make the mistake of renting a place long term without seeing it in person. Airbnb (http://www.airbnb.com/) is a good site to use for short term rentals. They have good protection for both renters and property owners, and you can get a good idea what a property is like by reading their reviews.

> *"I would NOT recommend renting long term online. A while back I rented from an online source for 5 days with a proviso it might be extended to a month—big mistake. We left after 3 days and I lost 2 days rent just to get out. The pictures were nothing like the facts. Many speculators here rent/lease cheap then flip and try to get tourist prices on a weekly base. Maintenance is usually non-existent."*

Houses are generally rented for one year where you pay the full year's rent up front. There is little to protect you legally if you run into problems, and it will be pretty much impossible to get any kind of refund if you change your mind about the property, or have any other kinds of problems. Occasionally, you can find rentals for six months or on a monthly basis, but these properties tend to be more targeted to the tourist market, so they can be a little more expensive.

If you go for a year long rental, it goes without saying that you need to check the place out thoroughly, almost to the level as though you were buying the property. Even if a property is brand new, you still need to check everything out, as sometimes the quality of workmanship can be a little shoddy.

Make sure you check the property out also at night. In Kuta/Seminyak it is fairly obvious where the night club areas are, but in Sanur there are a number of karaoke bars, or cafes as they are locally known, that are basically brothels, and can be very noisy at night, as this letter to the editor in the Jakarta Post highlights:

"My wife, two kids and I moved into a very nice neighborhood in Sanur and thought we had the perfect new home. But, the noise from the 'cafe' down the road seemed to get louder as the night went on. At 3 a.m., it still hadn't stopped or gotten quieter but had actually increased in volume. And so it has gone for the past week. Each night, the cafe gets louder and louder and doesn't stop until 3 a.m. or 4 a.m.

The other residents in our street tell us that they found it hard for a week or so but learned to sleep through the noise, kind of. As I ponder this predicament, I wonder what on earth we can do.

Moving again would be costly and inconvenient. Sound proofing against the incredibly loud and out-of-tune singing is not realistic. My mind continually returns to some sort of legal action or collaborative complaint by the people residing in the area.

And yet I have been in Indonesia far too long to expect anything but people to tell me to just put up with the situation. I thought I would move into this lovely neighborhood for many years and assumed that as my house is well over 500 meters and two streets away from the cafe, it wouldn't be a problem.

Are there noise pollution laws in Indonesia? Is there any limit to the times these cafes can operate and at what volume? Doesn't anyone think about the residents, working people and school children in the area when they crank up the volume at 3 a.m.? Am I going to be stuck with this problem and the frustration that there is no avenue of complaint for the next 12 months?"

I posted the above article on my blog, and someone posted this comment, which highlights another potential problem, which I am sure most people wouldn't even think about:

"We paid a year up front for a lovely villa in Canggu – when we arrived for the first night in our new home, it was right on dusk and there were a couple of bats inside the house (open living so we thought this as pretty normal) but as the night went on more and more kept coming. The house was infested with bats – every night, and they wouldn't leave until morning. I don't mean one or two – I'm talking 30 – 50 bats that fly into your heads. We couldn't leave bedroom doors open for more than one second, if we did we would have bats in our room that we would have to shoo out with the pool scooper! I have two small children and they were too scared to go to the bathroom at night as the bats also invaded the bathrooms. Not cool! We tried EVERYTHING to get rid of them – pest control, ceremony, smoking them out, mirrors hung from fishing line – everything! The owner wouldn't do a thing, so we had to leave a couple of months into our contract, losing all the money.

We are now very happily paying monthly in a home we love, I was glad to see more and more owners taking monthly payments – even if you end up paying a little bit more, I think it is worth it at the beginning until you know it is the home for you. Also, you don't really know a house thoroughly until you have lived in it through a wet season! A home can be lovely in the dry season and an absolute mess from November on!"

Some other things to check out when inspecting a rental property:

- Water pressure: Turn on the taps in the house. Check the pressure. Smell, but don't drink the water. Foul smelling water could be caused by a number of problems. Check if the water comes from a well/bore, or is it town water.

- Check the water heaters, if they are working as expected.

- Take note of how much electric supply you have. A typical villa may have around 5,000 watts. This is usually adequate to run several air conditioners, pool pump, refrigerator etc. Anything less than this and you could have problems using one or more high wattage appliances at the same time.

- Check the air conditioning units. They might need to be cleaned and re-gassed. It is cheap to get done, but you should get your landlord to organize it before you move in.

- Is the person showing you the property the actual owner? Or are they renting it and sub-leasing it to you? Some landlords could have a problem with this, so make sure you consult the real owner of the house.

- Look at the ceiling for water marks. It could be a sign of a leaky roof.

- Be wary of villas with *alang-alang* or grass roofs. It looks fantastic, but can be high maintenance and it tends to attract more insects and other critters.

If renting a house for one year and you have to pay for the rent in advance, I would suggest getting an agreement drawn up by a notary. The extra cost I think is well worth the money and can provide some protection for you.

House or Villa?

There is no clear definition between the two. You can generally expect anything advertised as a villa will be more expensive, and targeted towards foreigners. A villa will typically have a pool, open plan living areas and western style kitchens and bathrooms. Balinese houses will sometimes have the kitchen outside; a *mandi* for bathing, which is basically just a water storage place and you use a ladle to pour water over yourself, rather than a shower. The rooms in local houses also tend to be fairly small and dark, with little or no storage space. You can also find something between an expensive villa and a local house.

To Rent or Buy?

I would strongly advise to rent for at least one year, before even contemplating buying a house or land in Bali. It is also important to note, that foreigners cannot buy land in Indonesia. Some people get around the law by using a nominee—purchasing the property in the name of an Indonesian person. Long term lease (25 years) is another option and as a foreigner, you can put the lease in your own name.

7 EDUCATION – FINDING THE RIGHT SCHOOL FOR YOUR KIDS

One of the biggest decisions you face moving to Bali, is where to send your kids to school. It can also be one of the biggest expenses you face, especially if you plan to send your kids to an international school. All of the schools are different in their own way, and some schools may not be right for your child. Schools vary in their approach to discipline, character building, academics, work ethic and control of bullying.

Michelle shares her experience with schools in Bali:

"Our children have gone to two schools here in Bali, the first was an Australian International School which offers pre-kindergarten through to year 12. The school was very expensive, but had small class sizes, Australian teachers, Indonesian assistant teachers and academically it was a very good school with high standards. Our children improved and thrived with the smaller class sizes, which allowed a lot more one on one time with the teacher. Sadly, we couldn't keep up with the annual rising fees $20,000+ USD for two children.

The other school they are now attending, is a small independent school which offers a lovely feel of community and reminds us of what school was like when were children. At half the cost of the other school, it doesn't offer as much, but I don't think school is necessarily all about academics. We are happy here and the kids have made new friends, which is lovely. People must understand when they come to Bali, that schooling is expensive, without great facilities, but it is the wonderful multicultural experience the children get and I love that the teachers can give your kids a hug if they need one. Balinese people are caring and love children; I think western countries have made school to formal with ridiculous rules and regulations forgetting kids need to be kids and need more than just academics, but of course this is still very important. Dealing with such multiculturalism here makes for much flexibility."

If you would like your children to follow the curriculum of your country's education system, that will help to narrow your options. There are schools offering Australian, French and British based curriculum. There are also schools following Montessori and Steiner education philosophies.

The director of Pelangi School offers the following advice:

"Research and visit as many schools as you can, to find the one that is the best fit for your child and you. Ask people in the community. Contact the school and ask lots of questions. Which school do you feel takes the time and care, to best address your needs and concerns? What style of education do you want your child to have? There are excellent schools in Bali offering international standard education, you just need to decide which one best fits your needs."

The following are the main criteria which you will likely base your decision on.

Language

With regards to language, the choices you have include: English, Indonesian, Chinese and French. Local schools will also teach Balinese language, which might be important if one of the parents is Balinese. If you prefer your child to study in a different language, you may need to consider home schooling, or using a tutor.

Costs

International schools can cost between US$8,000 - US$16,000 per year, per child. Schools sometimes give a discount for more than one child studying at the same school. There are also usually additional charges, like exam and excursion fees.

Local schools are funded mostly by the government and are a fraction of the cost of an international school. They are an option, if your child can speak Indonesian fluently.

Location

As the traffic situation in Bali only worsens, location will be an important factor on deciding on a school. It could even be a good idea to decide on a school first and then find accommodation close to the school. Many people would consider you crazy if you say lived in Canggu, and sent your kids to a school in Jimbaran.

Home Schooling

Home schooling is another schooling option for parents living in Bali. There is much debate about the positives and negatives of home schooling, but if international schools are too expensive, or you are living in a remote location, it might be your only choice. Homeschooling requires a great deal of discipline and motivation, for both the student and you as the teacher.

There are many home schooling programs you can follow. Here are a couple of suggestions:

- SIDE, based on Western Australia's education: www.side.wa.edu.au

- Christian based education: www.mfwbooks.com

Natalie shares her home schooling experience:

> *"I'll be honest, I had no idea what I was doing! My lifesaver was a friend who had home schooled her children and put me on to a beautiful 1 year curriculum that was based around discovering other countries and cultures. It was perfect for us, and all the work was already done for me. The biggest hurdle was getting to a point of realizing that we didn't need to do EVERYTHING! Just the fact*

that we were living in a different country meant that the kids were constantly learning. Our youngest two were in kindergarten and Year 1 last year, so I figured learning to read and write and basic numeracy was what was important. Our year 5'er did lots of reading, spelling and we focused on mathematics. Our older son completed year 11 by distance education which is completely different from homeschooling.

His work was sent to him to complete and send back and he had access to his teachers via phone for oral examinations and any help that was needed. Fantastic! All the kids are back at school here in Australia, for the first term and are way ahead of the game which is very comforting. It's true, there's not the same type of respect for a parent as there would be for a school teacher, but hopefully we'll get better at that and overall the benefits, by far, outweigh this."

Indonesian schools

If your child speaks Indonesian fluently and the cost of international school is an issue, you may consider a local school. There are also religious based schools like Catholic or Muslim schools which are considered better by many Indonesians, than the state schools. The downside is that the education standard is very low and Indonesia ranks almost at the bottom of international tests, such as PISA (http://en.wikipedia.org/wiki/Programme_for_International_Student_Assessment).

Indonesian schools have the following levels:

Pre-school (TK)

Pre-school is not compulsory in Indonesia, but now most kids attend at least kindergarten. Most of the schools are privately run. From two years old, children can attend PAUD (Pendidikan Anak Usia Dini). From four, they can go to kindergarten (Taman Kanak-Kanak).

Primary School (SD)

Children attend primary or elementary school from around 6 years of age, for six years. It is known as SD, or Sekolar Dasar in Indonesian.

Middle School (SMP)

Students then move on to middle school or SMP, 'Sekolah Menengah Pertama', in Indonesian, for a period of three years.

Senior School (SMA or SMK)

After graduating from middle school, students can go onto a SMU or SMK school. SMU or Sekolah Menengah Umum (previously known as SMA) has more traditional academic subjects. SMK is for vocational studies, where students choose a specific field of study.

National Plus School

A National Plus school is a privately run school, that offers extended programs to the Indonesian national curriculum. The term 'National Plus' does not follow any laws or regulations, so it is open to interpretation by a school. There is an association for National Plus schools, but there is no requirement to be a member and being a member does not necessarily guarantee a certain standard— kind of typical of many things in Indonesia!

Pancasila

When discussing Indonesian schools, you might come across the word *pancasila*, with schools basing their teaching principles on it. Pancasila is the philosophical foundation of Indonesia, similar to the Bill of Rights in the United States. It comes from two old Javanese words, *panca* meaning five and *sila* meaning principles. The five principles are:

- Belief in one god
- Humanitarianism for all people
- National unity
- Democracy
- Social justice

International Schools in Bali

The following, is a guide to the international schools operating in Bali. You can use it to help you to narrow your decision to a few schools, which you can then visit and experience them for yourself.

Depending on the school, you might be able to allow your kids to attend the school for a few days, when you come to Bali for a holiday for example, so they can get a first hand feeling of what the school is like, before making any commitment.

If you are coming from Australia, it is important to note that the only school which starts the year in January, is AIS. The rest of the schools start the school year in July. Do not expect that you can enroll to a school and be admitted straight away. Try to enroll at least 1-2 months before you plan to move, as places are not always available. Also, give your kids time to adjust to Bali, before they have to start school. It would be too much to expect your kids to move to Bali, and start school straight away.

It is a good idea to have a backup plan for your school choice. Sometimes a school might not work out for whatever reason, so you should have a second choice available to you also.

The closest thing to a Tripadvisor for schools is the website, International Schools Review, (www.internationalschoolsreview.com/) which carries reviews of some of the schools in Bali. The reviews are written by teachers to help other teachers to evaluate international schools for seeking employment. There is a fee to access the reviews, but you do get something of an insight as to how the schools are perceived by teachers who actually worked there.

For people who are new to international schools, here are some of the terms you will come across.

IB – The International Baccalaureate is an internationally recognized program. The course leads to an IB diploma, which can be used to apply for universities and colleges around the world.

IB has programs for students from 3 to 19 years of age. It is divided into four programs:

- PYP – Primary Years Program, 3 – 12 years.
- MYP – Middle Years Progam, 16 – 19 years.
- Diploma Program, 16 – 19 years.
- Career-related Certificate (IBCC), 16 to 19 years.

IBO is non-profit educational foundation, based in Switzerland. See the International Baccalaureate Organization (IBO) for more information: www.ibo.org

CIE – Cambridge International Examinations, provides international exams and qualifications and was founded by the University of Cambridge in 1858.

The program is divided into:

- Cambridge Primary, 5 – 11 years
- Cambridge Secondary 1, 11 – 14 years
- Cambridge Secondary 2, 14 – 16 years
- Cambridge Advanced, 16 – 19 years

ABC Primary School

Location: North Kuta
Curriculum: British National
Website: http://abcprimaryschoolbali.com/

A non-profit primary school, that teaches British national curriculum.

Asian International School Bali

Location: Jimbaran
Curriculum: Cambridge University International Curriculum
Website: http://www.intschoolbali.com/

The Asian International School is a for profit school, based on Gandhian principles and caters to students from playgroup right through to senior high school.

The curriculum is based on Cambridge University International Curriculum.

Application forms are available from the school's website and prospective students maybe required to take a test or interview. Students come from more than 20 different countries.

The school year begins in July and goes through to June the following year.

Australian International School

Location: Kerobokan
Curriculum: Australian
Number of students: 210
Primary language: English
Curriculum: Australian national
Website: www.ais-indonesia.com

The Australian International School caters to preschool, primary and secondary students, and is not surprisingly, based on Australian curriculum. AIS Bali is one of four schools they operate in Indonesia.

The school follows the Australian school year, starting in January and finishing in December.

School fees range from US$2,250 for pre-school to US$10,350 for senior students. AIS Bali currently has 210 students. The campus is located in Kerobokan and set in lush, tropical gardens.

Extra-curricular activities include: sports such as: badminton, taekwondo, tennis and soccer. Other activities include: chess, origami, choir, IT robotics and dance.

Bali International School

Location: Sanur
Curriculum: PYP, MYP, IB
Primary language: English
Number of students: 330
Website: http://www.baliinternationalschool.com/

Bali International School (BIS) is one of Bali's longest established schools, taking in its first students in 1985. BIS caters to students from pre-school (3 years of age) right up to senior high school (grade 12). The school year starts in August and goes through to June the following year.

BIS offers three IB programmes: PYP, MYP and DP, in classes from pre-school to kindergarten all the way through to grade 12 graduation.

The school has approximately 330 students. Students come from over 30 different countries.

All of BIS classrooms are air-conditioned. The other facilities include: sports fields, an under cover sports arena, a 25 meter swimming pool, three science labs, a student support center, an art/technology block, a library with more than 30,000 volumes, two computer labs and a complete music suite with practice studios.

The fees range from US$4,000 per year for pre-school, up to US$17,300 for grade 11 and 12 students. There is also a capital levy charge and additional fees for the IB program.

Canggu Community School

Location: Canggu
Curriculum: UK Cambridge
Number of students: 400
Website: http://www.ccsbali.com/

Canggu Community School or CCS, started in 2001 and is an accredited Cambridge International Centre. The school caters to students from early years (3 years old) and up to year 13 (A levels). The school has access to the excellent sporting and recreation facilities of the Canggu Club. CCS aims to foster life long learning in students, to be socially responsible citizens and to be effective communicators.

The school year starts in mid-August and goes through to the end of June the following year. Parents should first take a look at the website and then contact the school to arrange an inspection. The school will arrange a trial visit and parents will be informed within 7 days if a place is available for their child.

For students in early year classes, the maximum class size is 20 students, 22 in Key Stage 1 (years 1 and 2) and 24 in Key Stage 2 (years 3-6) and upwards. CCS has a variety of music and sports programs for students.

School fees range from US$4,970 a year for pre-school to $10,625 for year 12-13 students. There are also additional fees for materials and resources and a capital levy.

Children's House

Location: Jimbaran
Curriculum: Montessori
Website: www.balichildrenshouse.com

Children's House is located on Jimbaran Hill and caters to preschool and primary aged children. The teaching is based on Montessori.

Dyatmika School

Location: Sanur
Curriculum: Cambridge
Number of students: 370
Website: www.dyatmika.org

Dyatmika School is conveniently located in Sanur. The school is an accredited Cambridge examination school and a National Plus school.

The school year begins in early August and goes through to mid-June. Dyatmika runs a playgroup for students from 3 years of age and has classes right up to senior high school. For admission, the school conducts interviews with the parents and has an entrance test.

Dyatmika is a fully accredited National School in Indonesia. The national curriculum is taught to all students from TKA (kindergarten) to class 8 combined with the International Cambridge curriculum. In class 9, students start to specialize in either the national curriculum with the International Cambridge curriculum, or just the International Cambridge curriculum. After the end of class 10, students must choose to follow either the National Curriculum for SMA, in 2 years, or the International Cambridge programme, consisting of AS levels and the A level exams which is also completed in 2 years.

All the Indonesian curriculum classes for the exams in classes 9 and 12 are taught by experienced and fully qualified National teachers. Students who sit these national exams are carefully prepared by these teachers. Upon successful completion of the national exams in class 12, students can apply to universities and colleges across Indonesia. Several Dyatmika graduates have gone on to Indonesian colleges and universities, mainly in Java. Students can choose the science option or the social sciences option for their SMA studies.

Dyatmika School is keen to practice the very best in teaching methodology. All the national teachers work closely with international teachers in the same subject area and material is presented to the students using the latest technology as well as with international standard teaching techniques. Many of our national teachers in the high school are bilingual and are therefore able to access many teaching resources in English. Dyatmika School is affiliated with teacher training colleges and universities in Bali and Java.

Dyatmika has 485 students from play group to high school class 12, with an average class size of 24 students.

The primary and secondary schools have separate facilities. The library for the primary school is
well stocked with fiction, non-fiction and reference books in both English and Bahasa Indonesia. The primary computer lab, is available for student use and all students are able to use the Internet for research and to access educational programs. There is one computer per student for all computer classes and mini labs beside each classroom for research. Smartboards are used in most of the primary classrooms. There are specialized music and art classrooms. Outdoor facilities include a sports field, an undercover area for sports and games and a separate primary school playground with adventurous, yet safely designed play structures.

The high school has recently been expanded. The classrooms are spacious and air-conditioned. The classrooms are equipped with various technology, including computers, LCD televisions, interactive whiteboards and e-beams. There are science labs, a library, specialized areas for the arts, music, sports as well as areas for the students to relax in the canteen or in the garden and verandah areas. The sports hall is a multipurpose covered sports facility, giving the school a full sized tennis court, basketball court, volleyball courts, badminton courts, an exercise/yoga room, shower facilities and an extensive covered seating area for spectators. Dyatmika also has a special area for counseling and employs a full time, experienced counselor who assists with careers guidance as well as personal counseling for all students.

The school offers a range of interesting extra-curricular activities, with something different each day. The primary school offers: Balinese dance, fun with science, art painting, karate, football (soccer), origami, jewelery making and violin. The high school has clubs for: cooking, photography, gardening, Chinese language (Mandarin) and drama.

Gandhi Memorial International School

Location: Renon
Curriculum: Indonesian or Cambridge
Primary language: Indonesian and English
Number of students: 1,000
Website: http://www.gandhibali.org/

The Gandhi Memorial International School (GMIS) opened in 2007, and aims to provide an international school experience, for an affordable cost. The school is located in Renon and is easily accessible to people living in Sanur.

The school year at GMIS has two semesters; mid-July until mid-December and mid-January until June. There are week long holidays for Galungan (Balinese new year) each semester. The school caters to students from kindergarten, right through to year twelve. To be accepted into the school, an interview with the principal is required, and students may need to take an entrance test.

The kindergarten is bilingual; English and Indonesian. This is followed by Indonesian primary, middle and high school, in preparation for national examinations, or Cambridge International Primary, followed by Cambridge Secondary, preparing for Cambridge Checkpoint, IGCSE and A levels.

The school has approximately 1,000 students from TK to SMA, with class sizes ranging from 20 to 28. The school has a high level of facilities, with air-conditioning and LCD projectors in all of the classrooms. They have a range of science, language and computer labs, full sized gymnasium, well-equipped library, music and art rooms.

GMIS has good opportunities for learning other languages with, French, Mandarin, Japanese and Indonesian offered in the international programme. The national program offers English and Chinese

(Mandarin).

The school places a great emphasis on promoting the principles of Pancasila (founding principles of Indonesia) and Gandhi. All religious and cultural events are celebrated throughout the year. The main goals for its students are developing a good character and providing the skills for further education.

EIF Bali (French)

Location: Kerobokan
Curriculum: French Baccalaureate and Toefl
Number of students: 275
Website: http://eifbali.com
Primary language: French
Approximate cost: US$6,000

EIF Bali is the obvious choice for French speaking families. The school is recognized by the French Ministry of Education and they are partners with AEFE, the French Agency for Education Abroad.

EIFB is part of a network of 480 schools around the world. It has the advantage of providing continuous education for your children, where you can easily relocate back to France or another EIF school in another country, without too much disruption.

All of the teachers at EIFB hold teaching qualifications certified by the French government. Class sizes are limited to 25 students per class. The school caters for students from 3 years of age (pre-school) right up to 17 years of age, in preparation to enter university. Half of the students are French citizens, half have mixed Indonesian and French parents, and a few come from Belgium, Switzerland and Canada.

The school year starts in early September and finishes at the end of June. Admission is generally automatic, providing a place is available. While the primary language of instruction is French, EIFB also provides English and Indonesian lessons.

The school's facilities include a 9,550 volume library, science lab, computer room and gymnasium. The school has access to the swimming pool at Canggu Club. The school is active in the Bali Schools Sports

Association (BSSA).

The school doesn't provide assistance with getting a KITAS, but students do not necessarily have to have a KITAS to attend.

The primary language of the school is French, but they also have English, Spanish and Indonesian language classes.. They have field trips in Bali and Indonesia, to visit volcanoes, rice fields and local schools. Students take part in Nyepi (Balinese holiday) celebrations, and the schools conducts Balinese dance and music lessons.

The extra-curricular activities the school provides, which are also open to children from other schools include: surfing, capoeira, oriental dance, football, badminton, drama, music, guitar, ukulele, basketball, extra French, extra English, extra maths and extra Indonesian language.

The school's goals for its students include: strong scientific skills, tri-linguism, computer literacy, team spirit and integration in a global world. EIFB's French Baccalaureate and Toefl program, can help students to gain access to all universities and colleges around the world, not just the French schools.

Green School

Location: Sibang (15 minutes from Ubud)
Curriculum: UK, Steiner
Number of students: 500
Website: www.greenschool.org
Primary Language: English
Approximate cost: U.S. $3,000 - $12,000 depending on schedule and age

No other school in Bali has received as much international media attention as the Green School, with some families moving to Bali just so their kids can go to the school. The school was founded in 2008 by John Hardy and his wife Cynthia. John Hardy is well known for starting a successful jewelery business in Bali, which he sold in 2007. The school is located about 15 minutes south of Ubud.

The Green School is not without its critics. Some people have questioned the safety aspect for example, of using bamboo for supporting structures, while others have been critical of the academic program. I cannot answer if the criticism is justified, but I do know that any kind of project that goes against traditional methods, particularly in education. and anything which involves children, is going to be put under the microscope.

John Hardy gave a TED talk which you can watch online here: http://www.ted.com/talks/john_hardy_my_green_school_dream.html
Reading through some of the comments you get an idea of some the controversy surrounding the school. The school has its detractors, but they seem to be a great deal more vocal, perhaps due to the mostly positive press the school has received. There is no doubt the school is based on a visionary concept, and since the school is still in its infant years, there is of course no way to judge the school as to how students will fare later in life. It might not be suitable for parents looking for a more traditional education for their kids.

The Green School is famous for being built from natural materials, including bamboo, mud and local grass. All of the bathrooms have compost toilets, which some parents have complained about the smell. The Green School gets about 80 per cent of its electricity from solar panels. They have a bird sanctuary for the Bali starling, which is currently on the brink of extinction. Vegetables are grown and livestock are raised on the school grounds, which are then used for school lunches. All organic of course!

Green School has two terms per year, one that starts at the end of August and the other at the beginning of January. The school caters for students from Pre-K (age 3), through to grade 12.

To apply for entrance to the school, you have to complete an application form and pay the application fee. For students in grade 6 and over, they need to write an essay of 400 words. The admissions team assesses each application, based on the information provided. An interview by Skype or in person, may also be required.

Green School has developed a unique curriculum based on the 'Three Frames of Learning'. It is a student-centered approach, with individual learning objectives. The three frames consist of thematic lessons, proficiency lessons and practical programs. The curriculum is designed to address the 'whole' of the child: spiritual, intellectual, emotional and kinesthetic. Each child has their own individual learning program and parents are encouraged to not ask. "How is my child doing?", but rather, "What is my child learning and how can I help them?"

The school had 320 students in August 2013, coming from over 40 different countries. The average class size is about 20 students. Around 30 per cent of the students come from Europe, 30 per cent from North and South America, 30 per cent from the Asia Pacific region and 10 per cent from Indonesia.

The school has a sports field, basketball gym, natural swimming pool, science labs, library and IT center. Every classroom has a garden for growing vegetables and a rice field, which students plant and cultivate. The classrooms do not have any walls and are designed so they always have a connection to nature.

The school can help provide support for obtaining visas.

The primary language of instruction is English, but the school teaches Indonesian to all of its students, so they can engage easily with the local community. French is available and they can provide support for other languages as required. Every class also has a dedicated Balinese teacher.

The school has a full sports program, where they also engage with other international schools. Sports include: football, volleyball, athletics, swimming and cross country. They also have a surf school program and the after school programs include: art, martial arts, music, drama and wood carving.

Green School's goal for its students, is to allow that spark to be allowed to grow so they can follow their own passions. They build a program that centers on the child and allows their skills to develop naturally. They aim to create 'green leaders' who can help to address the key issues facing the world.

Patricia tells her experience with Green School:

> *"Here is my perspective of the school. It is a private school. One of its focuses is sustainability - how to lead a sustainable lifestyle,*

how to live without excesses, how to care for the earth. Another of its focus is social entrepreneurship - how to identify an area with a need of a new business, how to develop the business so that it benefits the community you are working in/with, how to get the community involved and give back to them. It is also huge on community involvement - parents are expected to get involved in some way at the school (no effort is too small), they have free after school programs for kids from the neighboring local communities, they create opportunities for the older students to interact with the younger students for example through reading sessions, mentor ships, mini school on-site explorations led by the older students.

Although its approach to academics is not through rote learning (homework, memorizing, countless tests/pop quizzes), academics is covered through 'learning through experience'. For my husband and I, who believe that learning is a means to do something else (ie. you need to learn math to code, you need to learn to spell and read to write a story), this appeals to us.

There have been parents who place their kids in the school expecting something, and leave feeling disappointed. Some of the reasons for the disappointment include assuming that the school is a community school, insufficient focus on academics (tests, gradings etc), and inability of their kids to get used to the school culture. I feel that all these could have been avoided if parents had a clear idea of what GS is about before they enrolled their kids here. All schools have different approaches to education and learning, as do parents. It is important to find out whether the education and learning philosophy of the school gels with the education and learning philosophy that you as a parent has.

Don't be seduced by the hype of having your kids in GS before finding out whether it will suit your kid and your family.

My son wakes up on Saturday morning and asks to go to school. Is that a good indication of how he views school? Since being at GS, our kids also have a better appreciation of nature. They no longer feel that bugs like caterpillars or worms need to be crushed. They don't step on snails. They don't feel that dragonflies or fireflies are dangerous. They also don't pluck flowers off plants. If they see rubbish somewhere, they ask if they can pick it up to put in the recycle bin. They understand why we compost at home, and how the compost is good for plants. At home, we teach our kids to be as independent as possible. At GS, they also emphasis this. For example, they encourage the kids to clean up after themselves after a meal etc. But they also encourage working together. So they clean up together after play, after circle time, after a meal etc. These are the foundations of life skills, which my husband and I think are very important for kids to start learning from a young age.

One of the things we like about the school is its premises. It shows people that building and living gently on earth is possible. We also find that saying you are a GS parent identifies you, although we are not certain whether that is a good or bad thing because we are neither rich or entitled. We also appreciate that the teachers respect the parents' wishes in regards to healthcare. For example, some parents will request to be informed before medication is given, while others will insist not to give medication. Whatever is the case, the teachers or the nurse will inform the parents with a call or SMS, if something happens to their child.

Safety is also a very big thing at the school. When parents or helpers drop off the kids at school, the teachers acknowledge them by name, and always find an opportunity for the other kids to know that (example) pak Daniel is Elisa's father or ibu Wayan is Simon's helper etc. So there is a reduced danger of a stranger walking away with the kids. Of course, parents are requested to inform the teachers if someone else is picking up the kids. This is an added measure in case the teachers are busy, because the kids are always playing with each other. What we don't really like is the transient nature of the teachers and students. However, that is common in an international school regardless of which country it is in."

Another parent, Caroline shares experience with her son attending Green School:

"About two years ago we traveled to Bali for 2 months, absolutely loving it. The last week we did the tour at GS and when our son (then 1.5 years old) was playing in the Gecko classroom, my husband and I said to each other, "One day we will be back!" and so we did. We really like the fact that GS is doing things different. It is not perfect (where is?!) but the fact that they treat all

children the way they are, is something we really like. And the fact that all of the classrooms are outside, is great.

The word 'green' in Green School is sometimes interpreted differently, as say the word 'vegan' has different meanings and interpretations to different people. Also, it is sometimes seen as idealistic, but it really is a real school.

The positive points of the school are that the children learn things they would not learn in another school, such as environmental issues. Everything is done outside. There are more then 40 nationalities, and the students learn that everybody is different and everybody is the the same—a human being.

Some of the negative points: it's the jungle; so be aware of mosquitoes and other animals / diseases. Every semester people come and go. That's difficult for the families here long term, the constant coming and going in your class.

Our son was 3.5 years old when started at the Geckos, he didn't speak English, but after a few weeks he was able to communicate and now he speaks basic English. He likes it and it is also very intense. He goes three days a week and the days in between are to relax and chill at home. The driving of 30-45 minutes, one way is tiring for him. He likes all the songs and stories. He likes the relatively small class with 3 'Ibus' (Indonesian teachers), so a lot of attention. He likes the fact he has his own classroom, but is able to play with the other two classes (starlings and Kindy)."

High/Scope Indonesia

Location: Denpasar
Primary Language: English and Indonesian
Website: http://www.highscope.or.id/

HighScope Indonesia are based in Jakarta and have several schools throughout Indonesia, including Denpasar.

Highscope have education programs for children from one and a half years old right through to senior high school. The school year starts in July.

Highscope offers high school diplomas for students wanting to enter Indonesian universities or for students wanting to study abroad.

Some of the extra-curricular activities include: modern dance, computer gaming, movies, futsal (indoor soccer), Thai boxing and music.

Highscope's teaching philosophy is to train students to "think for themselves and not to accept the first idea that comes to them".

Jembatan Budaya School

Location: Kuta
Website: http://www.jbschool-bali.com/

Jembatan Budaya School is a National Plus school, teaching in three languages English, Indonesian and Chinese (Mandarin). The school was founded in 2004 and caters to students from playgroup to senior high school.

Class sizes are limited to 24 students per class. The facilities include air-conditioned classrooms, computer room, language and science labs, swimming pool, basketball court and play ground.

There are a range of extra-curricular activities including: sports, music, Japanese, scouts and journalism.

Montessori Bali

Location: Kerobokan
Curriculum: Montessori
Website: http://www.montessoribali.com/
Email: info@montessoribali.com
Phone: 0361 730 028

Montessori Bali offers an authentic Montessori program for students aged 3 – 14 years of age. Montessori has an emphasis on learning through discovery, with teachers as 'observers' rather than the traditional teacher-student style of education.

Pelangi

Location: Ubud
Curriculum: British/Indonesian
Primary language: English, with Indonesian taught daily
Number of students: 140
Website: http://www.pelangischoolbali.com/

Pelangi School is an independent, private, Indonesian School. Although the school is not technically an international school, most of the students come from outside of Indonesia and from mixed Indonesian/foreign parents. The school also has a mixture of foreign and Indonesian teachers. The school aims to maintain an Indonesian flavor, but deliver an international standard of education, in an environment that is natural, nurturing, holistic and in a small community context, where everyone knows each other.

Pelangi caters to students from playgroup (18 months) up to primary (elementary) school, grade 6 when the students are around 12 years of age. The school year begins around mid-August and goes through to end of June the following year.

Prospective students need to contact the school to check if a place is available. The director may meet with the family and if a student has special needs, for example if English is not their primary language, the school needs to assess whether they are able to meet the needs of each student, prior to admission.

Pelangi School follows a combination of IPC (International Primary Curriculum) and the Indonesian National Curriculum, delivered in an integrated format. The school believes in holistic education and the importance of education for the 'whole child'. Each class is taught by a foreign and Indonesian teacher.

Pelangi has around 140 students. The maximum number of students in a class is 22 and in grades 2-6, the maximum number is 25. The students come from a range of countries including Indonesia, Australia, Canada, America, Japan, Korea, Spain, France, Germany, Austria, Holland, Belgium, Denmark, Fiji, Taiwan, Italy, England and Italy. Pelangi literally means 'rainbow' in Indonesian and reflects the 'rainbow of nationalities' of its students.

Pelangi School is set amongst the rice fields in the town of Mas, about five minutes drive from central Ubud. New primary school facilities are currently being built. The school boasts extensive green, outdoor play areas, large classrooms and a school *warung* (restaurant).

The schools fees for 2013 are approximately IDR46,000,000 per year for primary school. There is also an enrollment fee of IDR6,000,000 for new students. The price goes down for the earlier grades. The school does not provide assistance for obtaining visas.

The school invites members of the community with special skills and talents to offer classes to students. For example, they have had African drum and dance classes, hip hop, art and currently creating opportunities to learn Balinese dance and art.

The goals of the school are to offer an international standard of education, that is nurturing and holistic, to succeed in a global community. The school aims to provide a solid educational foundation and teach students to become upstanding citizens with empathy, tolerance and respect for other people. The school also teaches students to have respect for the natural world, with a sense of social and environmental consciousness. The school understands that students learn in a variety of ways and aims to give them the freedom to grow, explore, inquire and build knowledge to best meet their needs.

Regents School Bali

Website: http://regentsschoolbali.com/
Email: info@regentsschoolbali.com
Address: Jalan Dewi Madri 58, Denpasar 80235

A new school located in Denpasar.

Sanur Independent School

Location: Sanur
Curriculum: Australian National Curriculum
Primary language: English
Website: http://www.balischool.com
Email: info@balischool.com
Approximate cost: US$990 – US$1,200 per term (4 terms per year)
Address: JL. Tukad Nyali Gg. SMU 6 No.3, Renon, South Denpasar -

Denpasar 80226, Indonesia

Sanur Independent School teaches students from kindergarten (4 years of age) to year 7 (13 years old). Their academic year starts in August and goes through to June. The school has four terms.

Admission is open to all nationalities, with at least a basic comprehension of English. The school conducts an interview with the student and parent. The parent must possess a KITAS (temporary stay permit) as well as the student (or at least in the process of applying for one). The school is able to support a student's KITAS application.

The curriculum is based on Australian National Curriculum with Civics and Bahasa Indonesia studies based on the Indonesian national curriculum.

Sekolah Lentera Kasih (SLK)

Location: Kerobokan
Curriculum: Cambridge
Primary language: English
Website: http://www.slkbali.com
Address: Jl. Gunung Salak No. 88 Krobokan Kec. Kuta Utara, Badung
Email: info@slkbali.com
Phone: 0361 900 2967

Sekolah Lentera Kasih or SLK is a Christian based school located in Kerobokan. It is a Cambridge International Center, and is affiliated with Lollypop Preschool. It is a small, community based school, with many students coming from mixed Indonesian and foreign parents. Many of the families are based long term in Bali, rather than on a short sabbatical.

SLK's school year starts in early July and finishes in early June. The school, along with its sister school Lollypop, caters for toddlers 1 and a half years old to prep. SLK caters for grade 1 (6 years old) up to grade 9, as of 2013/2014. Students will however be able to continue up to grade 12.

The school has an entrance test and interview. Each year the students sit international examinations. SLK is an accredited University of Cambridge International Examination Center. It is authorized to implement all Cambridge programs: primary checkpoint, secondary checkpoint, IGCSE and A level. SLK also offers national curriculum for Indonesian students.

The maximum number of students is 25 per class, with an average size of 16 students. Students come from many countries including: Indonesia, Australia, New Zealand, America, Canada, England, Germany, France, Japan, Korea, Holland, Spain, and others.

SLK is a modern, well equipped school, consisting of a three story building with air-conditioned classrooms, a modern state of the art bio-chemistry lab, and physics lab, well resourced library, new Apple Mac lab, music, art and Mandarin rooms. It has a multipurpose under cover court, 25 meter swimming pool, and small field.

All students learn Bahasa Indonesia, and the school has dedicated Indonesian as a second language class. Students study Mandarin and have the option in Grade 7 to continue studying. Bahasa Bali is part of the national curriculum. The school also has Balinese dance classes as part of it co-curricula activities.

The school does not provide sponsorship for KITAS.

The school's main goals for its students are academic excellence and character building.

Sunrise School Bali

Location: Kerobokan
Curriculum: British National Curriculum
Primary language: English
Website: http://www.sunriseschoolbali.com

Sunrise School Bali is a non-profit school, established in 2000 and is Bali's first 'holistic school'. The holistic education refers to an emphasis on individuality, creativeness and community focus. Some of the students' time is spent on community projects, like recycling and even a coral reef rehabilitation program.

The school caters to children aged from playgroup (age 3) to year 9. The school year is divided into four terms, starting on August 19 and going through to June the following year.

The school's curriculum is based on providing a holistic education and 'living values'. The academic foundation is based on British national curriculum. Every student is evaluated individually. Evaluation is done in an informal setting with teachers, where students spend a day or two in the prospective student's classroom.

Some of the extra-curricular activities include: basketball, Balinese dancing, capoeira and ceramics.

Taman Rama School

Location: Denpasar and Jimbaran
Curriculum: Denpasar – Cambridge, Jimbaran – National Plus
Primary language: English and Indonesian
Number of students: 1,000
Website: http://www.ourbalischools.com/
Email: info@ourbalischools.com
Phone: 0361 414849

Taman Rama School follows Gandhian principles as its guiding philosophy. It has two schools, one in Denpasar, which offers Cambridge curriculum and a National Plus school in Jimbaran.

The academic year has two semesters; mid-July until mid December and mid-January until mid June. There are week long holidays for Galungan, during each semester. The school caters for every school level from kindergarten right through to year 12.

With regards to the admissions procedure, students are required to attend an interview with the principal, and they may be required to take an entry test. Upon acceptance, you will then need to submit the necessary application forms and other documents. The school does not provide visa sponsorship.

The school offers education programs in both Indonesian and English languages. The kindergarten is bilingual. The school offers Indonesian primary, middle and high school to prepare for (Indonesian) national exams, or Cambridge International Primary followed by Cambridge Secondary, to prepare for Cambridge Checkpoint, IGCSE and A level exams.

The school has approximately 1,000 students. Class sizes range from 20 to 28 students per class.

The school has science, IT and language laboratories, a basketball and badminton hall, soccer field, swimming pool, art, music and dance rooms —as well as a library and meditation rooms. The school is a member of the Bali School Sports Association (BSSA). With regards to extra-curricular activities, the school offers: Balinese dance, first aid course, badminton, basketball, volleyball and scouts.

Other languages which the school teaches include French, Mandarin, Japanese and Indonesian as part of the international program. The national program offers English and Mandarin.

The school puts great emphasis on promoting the principles of Pancasila (philosophical foundation of Indonesia) and Gandhi.

Tri Hita Alam Eco School

Location: Denpasar
Curriculum: Singapore based
Primary language: English
Website: http://trihitaalam.com/
Email: info@trihitaalam.com
Approximate cost: PreK - IDR 750,000, K - IDR 1,000,000

Tri Hita Alam Eco School focuses on sustainable and environmental education. The school is attempting to "socialize the sustainable concept" through education, starting from an early age. They are subsidized by the Trihita Alam Foundation, to give international quality education, to local students.

The school has a pre-K to K2 classes, with elementary classes as the school progresses. Their school year starts in mid July and ends in early June.

Trihita Alam offers free trial classes for parents, so they can see whether they and their child feels comfortable and confident with the school's style of education.

Trihita Alam's philosophy is about connecting students with nature. Getting to know, love and to appreciate the nature around them in everyday life. Their students love to explore the birds, the fish pond and the school garden. Nature in everyday life, is their main syllabus. They use Singapore curriculum as the formal structure to support this green learning.

The school just started in 2013 and so far has 20 students registered. The class size is set at 15 students. They have just three classrooms right now, on 3,200 square meters of land.

Extra-curricular activities include: painting classes, Balinese dance and traditional Balinese music.

Pre-schools in Bali

Little Stars

Location: Sanur
Website: www.littlestarsbali.org
Email: littlestarsbali@gmail.com
Phone: 0361 285 993

Little Stars Bali is a preschool and kindergarten, that was established by parents and teachers to ensure quality learning, for children aged between 18 months and 6 years old. The school is located in a large, beautiful Balinese house, with a well equipped playground.

Little Stars has students from all over the world, but the highest proportion come from Australia, Indonesia and the UK. The school has between 80 and 100 enrolled students. Students may join anytime through the year, after they turn 18 months, but the maximum number of students is 100. Play group students, usually spend 2-3 days a week at the school. The class sizes are small and the ratio of teachers to students is inline with British curriculum guidelines.

English is used for instruction. Kindergarten students have Bahasa Indonesia classes as part of the curriculum. Little Stars believes in learning through play and inquiry and provides a range of opportunities for the children to develop their language, cognitive, motor and creativity skills. The school also gives a foundation in basic numeracy and literacy skills, which they do through fun activities and games. The curriculum is broad and balanced, that not only includes literacy and numeracy, but also incorporates other components, including art, craft, growing vegetables, cooking, science, sport and social skills.

The school is friendly, warm and caring. The teachers are well trained and motivated. They want the students to succeed and learn in a friendly and caring atmosphere. The school has merged the best aspects of the British curriculum, together with the best aspects of the Indonesian curriculum to give a culturally appropriate and international dimension to their program.

Cheeky Monkeys

Location: Sanur
Curriculum: British
Website: cheekymonkeysbali.com
Email: cheekymonkeysbali@gmail.com
Phone: 0361 282 420

Cheeky Monkeys is a popular pre-school with expats in Sanur. They offer a number of interesting and varied activities for kids, including: music, gardening and craft. The playground is quite spacious with plenty of trees for shade. In the afternoons, they offer some activities like ballet, dance and Silat – an Indonesian martial art.

Seminyak Spice

Location: Seminyak
Website: seminyakspice.com
Email: seminyakspice@gmail.com
Phone: 081514571738

Seminyak Spice is run by a Bristish/Indonesian lady, who has taught at international schools around the world, before starting her own school in Bali. They run classes for kids aged 16 months and up to 5 years old. They also run a Saturday club, afternoon sessions, a camp, and they can also cater for kids' parties.

8 HEALTH

With a combination of hot, humid weather, mosquitoes and different levels of hygiene than what you are probably used to; it is not surprising that you or your children will get sick at some point during your stay in Bali. Taking the appropriate precautions however, will help to reduce the risk.

At least one or two months before you move to Bali, get a complete medical check up from your doctor. You may also wish to consult with a doctor that specializes in travel medicine to get the required injections and inoculations, that you will need to travel to Bali.

Typhoid

Typhoid fever is a bacterial disease, that can be passed by someone who goes to the toilet and then touches food, without washing their hands. The infection is passed through contaminated food. Even though the terms typhoid and typhus are sometimes confused in Bali, they are caused by different kinds of bacteria. Typhus is passed by human body lice or rat fleas and has different symptoms from typhoid.

Typhoid's symptoms include high fever, cough, abdominal pain and diarrhea. Vigilant hand washing after going to the toilet and before handling food, is the best way to control the disease.

Dengue Fever

Dengue fever is common in Bali, particularly during the rainy season. It is spread by mosquitoes. Symptoms include fever, head ache, muscle and joint pains. In a small number of cases, it can be life threatening. Children may experience symptoms of the common cold with vomiting and diarrhea A blood test can check for the virus.

There is no vaccine for dengue fever and prevention basically means avoiding getting bitten by mosquitoes. Covering the skin with clothes and mosquito nets are a couple of ways to prevent getting bitten. Avoid stagnant water to accumulate around your house and neighborhood to stop mosquitoes breeding. Debris like plastic containers and old tires, that accumulate water, need to be disposed of.

Drinking guava juice is said to make you feel better if you happen to contract dengue fever.

Rabies

Rabies reached its peak in Bali, around 2011. It has somewhat come under control, but you still need to be very vigilant around dogs. If you or your child gets bitten by a dog, you need to immediately wash the wound with warm, soapy water for 10-15 minutes. Then go to the nearest hospital to get the required vaccination.

If you have a dog, you should make sure you get your dog vaccinated against rabies. It is a good idea to find out if your neighbor's dogs have also been vaccinated. Many villages can provide free vaccinations for dogs. Not all dogs show the classic symptoms of foaming at the mouth. Other symptoms include a dog becoming quiet and passive or unsteady walking.

BARC (Bali Adoption and Rehabilitation Center) can provide information and advice on rabies and anything animal or pet related in Bali: www.balidogrefuge.com

Head Lice

Head lice is a common problem with children in Bali, perhaps due to the humidity and warm climate. Head lice are extremely contagious and can be easily passed through sharing of combs, clothes or hats.

Head lice can be treated by combing out the lice and eggs with a steel 'nit comb', which you should bring with you as they are not available in Bali. There are also some shampoos and chemicals which you can use to treat head lice, but may not be available in Bali. Tea tree oil is available and can be used to treat and prevent infestations, by adding a little to your shampoo.

Snakes

Snakes are common all over Bali. While some are venomous, bites if treated quickly are not lethal. The venom acts like a nerve poison, paralyzing its victim. If someone is bitten they need to be taken to hospital and put on a respirator, to help with breathing until the toxin wears off. Snakes are typically shy and will generally only attack if provoked.

For more information on snakes and what to do if you find them in your house, check out Ron Lilley's Facebook page: www.facebook.com/ronlilleysbalisnakepatrol

Climate

If you are coming from a cool climate, moving to Bali might take some time to adjust to the tropical weather. It is important to stay hydrated, by drinking plenty of water. Coffee, tea and alcohol make you urinate more, so you will need more water to compensate. The tap water in Bali is not fit for drinking, so you need to buy bottled water. 'Aqua' and 'Cleo Water' are the most common brands.

Bali basically has two seasons, wet and dry. Wet season goes from around October to March. It rains every other day, often in the afternoon and there are usually a few big storms where it constantly rains. Fortunately, typhoons don't reach Bali.

Health Insurance

It is imperative for every person visiting or living in Bali to get adequate health insurance. Bali's health care and hospitals have improved tremendously over the past few years, but they still have a long way to go before they meet first world standards.

Anyone involved in a serious accident or requires major surgery, will generally have to go to a hospital in nearby Singapore or Australia. It is for this reason that your insurance should cover emergency evacuations, sometimes referred to as 'medivac'.

There are fairly frequent stories in the media, about foreigners who have a motorbike accident, and don't have travel insurance. Their families are then left to try and raise around US$60,000, which is the money required—just for the evacuation.

The cheapest option is travel insurance, and some companies even offer coverage for periods of up to 12 months. It might be adequate if you are living in Bali just for one year. If however, you develop some kind of illness, you might not be able to renew your policy the following year.

Then there are international insurance companies that provide insurance to people living overseas, such as Allianz and BUPA and policies can be purchased in Bali.

If you plan on riding a motor bike, be sure that your insurance covers you for it, in the case of an accident. Usually there will be something specific in the fine print, whether you require a local driver's license to be covered. An international license might not be adequate for insurance purposes. Be sure to check your policy thoroughly.

Hospitals and clinics

BIMC Hospital

BIMC is the most well known hospital in Bali, and provides international standard of care for expats and tourists. They were recently taken over by Siloam Hospitals.

Web: www.bimcbali.com

Phone: +62 361 761 263

International SOS Clinic

International standard hospital located in Kuta, that also offers first aid training.

Web: www.sos-bali.com

Phone: +62 361 710 505

Kasih Ibu

Web: www.kasihibuhospital.com

Phone: +62 361 223 036

Prima Medika

Hospital located in Denpasar, with branches in Nusa Dua and Ubud.

Web: www.primamedika.com

Phone: +62 361 236225

Puri Bunda

Web: www.puribunda.com

Phone: +62 361 437 999

International Tourist Medical Services

Provide emergency medical care and evacuation services.

Web: http://www.itmsbali.com/

Phone: +62 361 751981

Siloam Hospital Bali

One of Bali's newest and modern hospitals. Siloam Hospital seem to have their eyes set on the lucrative Asian medical tourism market, offering a range of medical services, including cosmetic and dental packages.

Web: www.siloamhospitals.com

Phone: +62 361 779 911

Surya Husadha General Hospital

Focuses mainly on internal medicine.

Web: www.suryahusadha.com

Phone: +62 361 233 787

Dentists

While Bali's medical care might be lacking, Bali is becoming popular for tourists to have dental work done while on vacation. These three places are popular with tourists and expats.

Bali 911 Dental Clinic

This clinic is conveniently located in Bali Galleria shopping mall.

Website: www.bali911dentalclinic.com

Phone: +62 361 766 254

Dr Indra Guizot

Phone: +62 361 222 445

Dr. J.R. Wijaya

Phone: +62 361 742 1817

Chiropractor

Global Health Center

Web: globalchiro.asia/our-clinic/bali-clinic

9 COST OF LIVING

South east Asia has long been a popular destination for tourists and expats Not only for its culture and warm climate, but also for its cheap cost of living. Indonesia of course falls into this category. With the surge in the popularity of Bali for both international and domestic tourists, however, the cost of living has risen quite dramatically over the past few years, especially in the south of Bali.

The three biggest expenses for a family will typically be: housing, education and health insurance. If you are negotiating working conditions with an employer to work in Bali, I would suggest trying to get these included, or at least partially included, in your contract.

Housing

It is not easy to give a guide to housing rentals in Bali. Like real estate anywhere in the world, the location is going to have a big influence. Anything within walking distance to the beach for example is going to be expensive. A typical 3 bedroom villa in Seminyak with pool, might cost around 150-160 million rupiah per year. Prices in Ubud have skyrocketed recently, as it has become a very popular place for expats.

Having said that, if you are prepared to spend the time looking and don't mind living a bit outside of the tourist areas, you can find much cheaper places, especially if you can deal and negotiate directly with the owner. Renting for multiple years you can get a reduction in rent, but of course you will then be locked in for a longer period.

Education

I have included the prices for some of the international schools in the education section. Bali International School for example costs US$4,000 per year for pre-school, up to US$17,300 for the senior years. This is per child, but most schools give a bit of a discount for additional children. There may also be other charges and levies, like an enrollment fee.

Insurance

Health insurance is a must for anyone living in Bali. This can cost around $500 for travel insurance (for one year) and up to $5,000 a year for more comprehensive insurance.

Transport

For getting around you will need your own car. Many foreigners get around on motorbikes in Bali, but this is not very practical for a family. To rent a family car like a Toyota Avanza, the price will be about 3 million rupiah per month. If you plan on living in Bali for a year or more, it will probably work out cheaper in the long run, buying your own new or second-hand car. A second-hand car, say about 3-4 years old, should cost around 100-150 million rupiah. New car prices start at around 200 million rupiah. An automatic scooter, such as a Honda Vario should cost around 500,000 rupiah a month to rent and about 13 million rupiah to buy new.

Food

The good news about food, is that it is generally cheap and should be less than what you would pay in most western countries. The bad news however, is that anything imported, is usually more expensive. Wine and spirits are also more expensive because of the high import duties. If you have friends visiting you regularly from overseas, you can ask them to buy your favorite beverages duty-free.

Eating out is one of the joys of living in Bali. Some places have quite a social atmosphere and are a good way to meet other people. Restaurants can range from road side warungs serving $2 plates of nasi goreng, right up to fancy places with Michelin star chefs and everything in between. Many families hire a *pembantu* or maid to help prepare meals. Most will be eager to learn how to make your favorite dishes.

A very rough budget for a family of three, would be about US$500 a month, with a couple of dinners out at modest restaurants.

Internet

Telkom Speedy, which is the only ADSL internet provider in Indonesia, has packages ranging from around $50-$100 a month depending on the speed. 3G services, such as XL, 3 or Smartfren are cheaper and a good option if you are on the move, but service can be patchy and speeds can slow to a crawl during peak times.

Electricity

With the ongoing building and hotel boom in Bali, the demand for electricity has similarly increased, with rates becoming more expensive each year. Pay-as-you-go meters which have become the norm in Bali, are reportedly more expensive than meters where you get a monthly bill. You also pay a higher tariff depending on the VA power supply.

A house or villa with multiple air-conditioners, water heaters, pumps pool filters and other large consumers of electricity will require a larger VA power supply. The PLN (electric company) has a simulator on their website, which you use to get an idea of how much electricity you will have to pay: http://www.pln.co.id/eng/ It costs approximately 800 rupiah (about 80 cents) per hour to run an AC.

Visa Costs

If you are working for a company, they will take care of your visas. If you are married to an Indonesian citizen, the spouse visa is about 750,000 rupiah per year, if you apply yourself. Going through an agent will be considerably more. The retirement visa is approximately 6-7 million rupiah per year.

If you plan to use a social visa, you need to renew it every month. Doing it directly through immigration is around 250,000 rupiah per month. An agent will charge about 500,000 to 600,000 rupiah per month, per person.

Now, the social visa is good for a maximum of six months, so if you plan on staying longer than that, you will need to exit the country and apply for a new visa at an Indonesian consulate or embassy. Most people opt for Singapore, as it is the closest flight to Bali. So you need factor in the costs not only for the new visas, but also for flights and hotel. So you would need to budget for around $1,000 every six months, for flights and hotel for a family of three.

Staff Costs

Most foreigners living in Bali employ at least one person, typically a *pembantu* or maid. The minimum salary is currently around 1.3 million rupiah per month. Although most people would pay more than this.

Other Costs

I have included the basic expenses. Other expenses will include fees to register in the *banjar* or village you are living. There are fees for rubbish disposal, which are also dependent on the village you are living in.

Then there of course other costs such as entertainment and sports activities. A Canggu Club membership can cost several thousand dollars, with additional monthly fees.

10 FINDING WORK

I wish I had a dollar for every time someone has asked me how to find a job in Bali. The emails that I get, usually go something like this: "I have worked in HR for a multi-national company for 20 years and I have an MBA. What is the best way to find a job in Bali?"

Unfortunately, there are few jobs available in Bali to foreigners. If you are looking to move to Bali to find work to support your family, you will more than likely be very disappointed. It is often said the Bali is a good place to spend money, but a difficult place to make money.

It is very expensive for a company to employ a foreigner. Just the cost of the working visa is around US$2000 a year and the company needs to get approval from the Department of Manpower to employ foreigners.

There are some opportunities in the hospitality industry in senior management positions and as a chef, in upscale restaurants and five star hotels. There are a couple of companies that employ English teachers, but the salaries are quite low at around $800 a month, and wouldn't be enough to support a family; it is about the bare minimum for a single person to live. There are good opportunities at international schools for qualified teachers. Some foreigners work as scuba dive instructors, but the salary is apparently very low and some companies don't even bother organizing a working visa.

In 2011 there were 1,455 working permits issued to foreigners in Bali according to the Bali Discovery website, but of course it doesn't take long to realize there are many more living here, so what does everyone do for income?

I would say the majority of foreigners living in Bali earn their income outside of Bali, either through savings and investments, or through an overseas business that they run remotely. As mentioned in the introduction, there is a growing number of fly in-fly out workers, who hold a job overseas, usually in mining or on an oil rig and spend their off days in Bali, usually while their families live full-time in Bali.

Starting a business is another option. Like starting a business anywhere in the world, it can take considerable time, before it starts to make a profit. The expats who are running successful businesses in Bali, have usually spent many years building them up.

If you are looking for ways to supplement your income, I would suggest first looking at ways you can find customers from your own country, using your existing skills and knowledge. Such as technical writing, graphic design or maybe online coaching.

Some foreigners move to Bali and their first idea for a business is a restaurant or bar, even though they have no previous experience, unfortunately often with disastrous results. Take things very slowly before making any big financial decisions in Bali.

11 MANAGING STAFF

When it comes to employing staff in Bali, there are no hard and fast rules, so I would like to share some of my personal experiences. When my wife and I first moved to Bali, we didn't feel the need to employ any staff. We lived in a small house and weren't working, so didn't mind taking care of everything by ourselves. Even when we started a business we employed staff only for the business and we still took care of our own house. That all changed after the birth of our son.

I first suggested to my wife that we should hire a *pembantu* or housekeeper for three months or so as we got used to the extra work taking care of a baby. Almost two years later, Ketut our pembantu, is still working for us, and now I could not imagine life without her.

In my previous working life, I never had to manage people, so employing staff has been a new experience for me. Actually, I am very happy to leave the hiring and firing to my wife. While it is great having staff to help around the house, it is not always easy managing them. Different culture, different education and just a different way of doing things can sometimes be frustrating, but it will also sometimes give you a laugh—or make you cry.

We run a small guest house and employ a range of staff, including cooks, cleaners and drivers. In general we have had mostly positive experiences with our staff. Of course it is not all plain sailing, and we have had to let a couple of people go. It is not something you want to do, but if it is only making your life more stressful, then sometimes it is inevitable.

Everyone has their own style of management. I am an easy going person, so I have always struggled to be firm with people, and taken the view that I wouldn't ask anyone to do anything I wouldn't be prepared to do myself. Some people tend to be too easy going and you will find that your staff take advantage of this, and others act like a dictator, yelling and screaming at their staff. You need to find balance between being easy going, and strict with your staff.

Types of jobs

The following is a list of some of the main types of jobs people employ staff for. It does not necessarily mean that you will have one person for each job. If your garden is not large, you could have your security guard for example, do some gardening.

<u>House keeper (pembantu)</u>

If you only employ one staff member, you will more than likely employ a pembantu, or house keeper. A good house keeper will have your place running like clockwork. Their general duties include cooking, cleaning and helping with your children.

They might also do shopping, or pay your bills. If they do not have previous experience, you may need to provide them with some training, particularly with electronic appliances like washing machines or dish washers.

Balinese also have different levels of hygiene and cleanliness, so if like your house to be cleaned in a certain way, you may need to teach them. One thing Balinese seem to love doing is sweeping the leaves outside. Whether it is your drive, grass or garden beds, they sweep up every leaf.

It was difficult for me to get used to, as the leaves provide good natural mulch in the garden. The thing which will puzzle you, is that even though all of the leaves get swept up, you will still find plastic wrappers and cigarette butts everywhere. While your staff will learn some new skills, old habits are hard to break!

Cook (Juru masak)

If you have a large family or would like to have a greater variety of dishes, you may consider hiring your own cook. You might be lucky to find someone who has restaurant or hotel experience. Cooks generally do the grocery shopping and they can also cook for your other staff and prepare your child's school lunches. Balinese generally tend to use more sugar and oil than necessary in their cooking. Some even use MSG, so even if they have experience, you might need to provide some training.

Driver (Sopir)

Considering Bali's crazy traffic, you might consider hiring a driver. Drivers can take and pick up your kids from school and they are also usually responsible for washing the car and ensuring it is maintained.

Gardener (Tukang kebun)

If you have a large garden, or would like to grow your own fruits and vegetables, you might consider employing a gardener. I am sure most guys say they can work as a gardener, but few actually have any kind of knowledge of things like mulching and making compost.

Bali Eco can provide the materials and training for your staff on how to make compost. It is common in Bali for people to use harmful pesticides and chemicals to control garden pests. If you want to have an organic garden, which is safer for your family and pets, you might need to provide some training and assistance on how to implement this.

Security (Satpam)

There are frequent reports of villas getting robbed. It is particularly a problem with villas located in isolated locations. If you are living in such a place, you might consider getting a security guard. Having a security guard may provide something of a deterrent, but it is not uncommon for them to fall asleep during the night. They may even run away, if they are confronted. It is a good idea to employ someone from your local village, to be your security guard.

Finding Staff

It is easy finding staff in Bali, the challenge is finding honest and hard working people, that you can get along well with also. While there are some places on the internet to find staff, the best way is usually through personal recommendations.

Let your friends know you are looking for staff, and you will soon have people knocking on your door, looking for a job. Your village will prefer it if you employ people from the same village. This is not always easy however. If you hire a security guard, I would suggest employing someone living in the area.

Some villas and large homes, will have living quarters for your staff. These are usually small rooms somewhere at the back of a property, separate from the main house. If your staff does not live locally or even comes from a different island, you may consider having them live in your house. This is a fairly common situation in Indonesia and the staff will be happy that they have a place to live.

I would suggest putting all staff on a probation period of three months. This gives you the opportunity to see how well they work before committing to a longer contract.

Communication

Communication really is the key to a successful relationship with your staff. Being able to speak the same language whether it is English or Indonesian, obviously is important. The main thing is to try and make it clear as possible, what is expected of your staff and how you would like things to be done.

It is important to make this very clear, right from the beginning. It can be difficult to change things later. Establishing some kind of routine makes things easier to manage, as they will know exactly what is expected of them each day, whether you are there to supervise or not. You may even consider making a list of tasks and pinning it on the wall.

Work Schedules

Discuss and agree on start, finish time and holidays during the interview process. The expression 'jam karet' is often used in Indonesia, literally meaning 'rubber time'. Make it clear that you would like your staff to be punctual. Five minutes late, can quickly turn into 30 minutes if you are not too careful.

Balinese staff will take time off for important ceremonies like Galungan, Kuningan and Nyepi. It is important to discuss this in the interview process, as to how often they need to take time off for these and other ceremonies.

Salary

The minimum worker's salary in Bali is around 1.3 million rupiah. In large cities and the main tourist centers, the expected salary will be more than this. People with previous experience and English speaking ability, will usually expect a higher salary.

Employers in Indonesia usually provide meals for their staff. This could be food they prepare themselves at your place, or extra money which they use to buy their own food. After you have employed someone for more than one year, you are expected to pay them one month extra salary as a bonus.

Terminating staff

One of the most difficult things you face with employing staff, is firing them if there is a problem, or things just aren't working out. It is not a pleasant experience for both parties. As previously discussed, communication is the key. Make sure you are very clear what is expected of your staff and what kind of behavior is unacceptable. Avoid letting problems linger for too long.

You may find staff members lose interest in their job and while they might not ask to resign themselves, they might start doing their jobs sloppily. They might be reluctant to resign themselves as their family might get upset if they make the decision to quit.

If you are having problems, I would suggest giving three warnings. Explain clearly their mistake and see if the situation improves. If the person was recommended to you from a friend, discuss the problem with your friend. They might be able to talk with your staff. Usually your friend will be understanding and will support your decision, if you explain everything clearly.

12 GENERAL AND USEFUL INFORMATION

Banjar System in Bali

If you are planning on living in Bali, I can recommend getting to know the basics of how the local government and society works. In Bali, daily life revolves around the *banjar*. A banjar is a small village or hamlet.

The banjar is made up of all of the adult, married men in the village. While the men deal with the regulations and organization of the banjar, the women deal with preparing the offerings for ceremonies. Once a man's sons have become adults and married, the father can retire from his banjar responsibilities.

Banjar members are responsible for building and maintenance of roads and buildings, security, settling disputes, preparing food (not cooking) for ceremonies, building the structures used in cremations, and ensuring compliance with the village rules. The banjar members meet every 35 days. If a member is not able to be present they are required to pay a fine. Banjar rules are written on lontar leaves and stored in the village temple. Infraction of these rules can lead to heavy fines or refusal for individuals or families to participate in village ceremonies. The head of the banjar is called the "Kelian Banjar".

"Pecalang" provide the security for the village and you will see them directing traffic at ceremonies. They can be recognized by their black and red uniforms.

The banjar owns the property that lies between houses, the streets and ditches, and public buildings. If a person in the banjar dies without an heir, their property is transferred to the banjar. Until recently only sons could inherit their father's property. In 2010 the law was changed allowing daughters to inherit a portion of her father's land if there are no sons.

As well as the banjars, there are also subak, or irrigation societies. The subak organization is responsible for ensuring that all the water in the irrigation system that feeds the rice fields is distributed fairly across the island. These associations were founded more than 1,000 years ago with the first reference to them in 1022.

There are around 1,300 subak organizations across Bali with each one having about 200 members. Everyone who owns land must be a member of their subak and pay membership fees. Everyone who is a member must attend monthly meetings. Everyone within the subak organization is equal, regardless of their caste. A head is referred to as the "Kelian Subak", and together they will make the decisions about when rice will be planted and harvested, when to make offerings, how dams and ditches will be repaired, and what fertilizers or pesticides are to be used.

Telephones and mobile phones

If your house doesn't already come with a land line telephone, you could have trouble getting one connected. Most people just rely on mobile phones, but a telephone line can be good if want to get an ADSL internet connection. If you don't have a telephone line, but still want to have a regular telephone in your house, one alternative is a Flexiphone. It could be a good idea to have for your staff or kids to use and they don't have mobile phones. It looks like a regular phone and you get a 03 number, but works as though it is a mobile phone.

Mobile phones in Indonesia are generally sold 'unlocked'. If you are bringing a mobile phone from your country, there is a good chance that it is locked to a provider in your country, but this can be unlocked in Bali.

You can then choose which provider you want to use.

For mobile phones, you have the option getting a pre or post-paid phone. Most people in Bali have pre-paid phones, where they buy a SIM card and then they purchase credit or 'pulsa' when they need it. This is a good option as you don't have to worry about paying bills, but it can sometimes be a bit inconvenient having to top up your credit all of the time.

The 'post-paid' option is where you get a bill every month, based on the previous month's usage. This option is only available to Indonesians or KITAS holders.

It is difficult to say exactly which mobile company will best suit your needs. The providers often have various promotions and discounts when you call someone on the same network. So if all of your friends are using one network, you might want to choose the same.

Depending on proximity to a mobile tower, coverage will vary. Again check which provider works well in the area you will be spending the most time. New towers seem to be going up all over the island, so coverage has definitely improved over the past few years.

Mobile phone shops are everywhere in Bali selling 'pulsa' and mobile phone accessories. The most concentrated stores can be found along Jalan (road) Tekur Umar in Denpasar.

Here is a list of the telephone providers in Bali:

- Indosat: www.indosat.com

- Flexi: www.telkomflexi.com

- Telkom: www.telkomsel.co.id

- XL: www.xl.co.id

Internet

Internet speed is an eternal source of frustration for foreigners living in Bali, many of whom are probably used to high speed broadband and fiber networks. Several options are available including ADSL, radio transmitter and mobile networks.

Generally speaking, Telekom Speedy ADSL internet, which operates over a fixed telephone line is the most reliable. Of course you always hear people complaining that the service is not so 'speedy'. They have several packages available depending on the speed you want.

If you don't have a telephone line, your next option is using a radio transmitter. This usually involves installing an antennae on your roof with a transmitter. Several internet providers offer this service, with most offering the service just to a few particular areas. As with selecting a suitable mobile phone company, get recommendations from your friends living in the same area as you.

Bali also has a 3G mobile service which you may consider, especially if the above two options are unavailable. There are a variety of plans available that tend to change constantly with various promotion packages. Many mobile shops simply 'cut' the usual SIM card for iPhone/iPads. The quality of the mobile service varies on many factors, but tends to work well in the major tourist centers. The speed is generally adequate for checking email and web browsing and is a good option for when you are traveling, but in my opinion not reliable enough for a permanent solution.

Internet Providers

Neuviz

Tel: 0361 847 5626 / 0361 921 2439

Website: www.neuviz.net.id

Global Xtreme

Tel: 0361 736811

Website: http://www.globalxtreme.net/

Blueline

Tel: 0361 769 353

Website: www.blueline.co.id

Indosat M2

Tel. 0361 300 3000

Website: www.indosatm2.com

Telkom Speedy

Website: http://telkom.co.id

Home Security and Personal Safety

Home burglaries are a fairly common problem in Bali. Robbers tend to work in gangs, breaking into homes while their occupants are sleeping. Villas located in remote areas, especially in rice fields are often a target. Locals are as much of a target as foreigners.

There are various precautions you can take, but I don't think there is one fail safe solution. Dogs are a good deterrent. Hiring a security guard, or *satpam* is another option, but how can you make sure they do not just fall asleep or even run away if there is any trouble? Steel bars on windows can be effective, as well as strong locks on doors.

Making friends in your neighborhood and local community, will help you to keep aware if there are any problems with break ins in the area and neighbors will help to look out for your property. Perpetrators tend to come from outside of the area.

When there is construction work going on, using workers from outside of Bali, that can be a potential problem. Be very careful who you let into your house, especially when it comes to anyone doing construction or maintenance to your house. Use only people that have been recommended by others and preferably live in the local area.

Keep expensive items like laptops and iPads hidden away. Don't keep large amounts of cash in your house, and consider renting a safety deposit box at a bank to store your valuables. A safe is an option, but it could also make someone think you might be keeping something very valuable. Thieves are generally not going to be interested in stealing things like your passport, so in my opinion they don't need to be locked away in a safe.

Banking and Finance

In principle you need to have a KITAS to open a bank account in Indonesia. Although many people report now that they can open a bank account if they have an introduction from an existing customer from the bank.

Having a local bank account can help save on ATM fees, as withdrawals from an overseas bank can get expensive. It is also useful for paying bills, and generally making your money more accessible. ATMs can be found easily all over the island and withdrawals can be made from all major international card networks.

In some countries, it is common for ATMs to give the card back first and then the cash, but in Bali, ATMs usually give the cash first and then your card, making it easy for people to leave the ATM with their cash, but forgetting their card. If this happens contact the bank immediately to retrieve your card from the machine.

It is a fairly simple process to open a bank account—you just need to show your passport and KITAS. If you do not have a KITAS, some banks may still allow you to open an account if you are introduced by another customer. There are many large banks to choose from such as BCA, Mandiri, BNI and Permata. It is not easy to recommend one particular bank over another. The Australian Commonwealth Bank has branches in Bali and might be an option for existing customers or Australians living in Bali.

Internet banking is just getting started in Indonesia and it is useful for paying bills online such as internet, telephone and satellite television subscriptions.

Credit Cards

Indonesia is still very much a cash based society, and only larger stores, hotels and restaurants accept credit card payment. Many places charge an additional 3 per cent fee for using a credit card. As a foreigner it is unlikely an Indonesian bank will issue you with a credit card, unless you have an equal amount of savings in your account.

Electricity

Bali has experienced huge growth in the past few years, especially in the tourism sector. Unfortunately, basic services like electricity has struggled to keep pace with the demand. Power outages are fairly common, but they generally do not last for more than a couple of hours. It is a good idea to keep a stock of candles and flashlights on standby. Some homes have diesel or gasoline generators, which they run during such times.

All new homes in Bali are now fitted with 'pulsa meters'. So instead of getting a bill to pay, you need to purchase credit, or pulsa in advance. Make sure to check the wattage of your house before you rent it. If the electricity does not have high enough wattage, you might not be able to run several electrical appliances at the same time, like air conditioning units or electric ovens.

The electricity bill can be paid through a bank or at an ATM. To find out the cost of your bill, you can call 108-123 (English) or 123 (Indonesian), or you can check it online at: www.pln.co.id. Look for 'Cek Tagihan Rekening'. Just enter your 10 digit customer code. The bill is due to be paid before the 20th of each month.

Post

When we first moved to Bali, we lived in a fairly remote village and since even our neighbors were unsure of their postal address, we decided to rent a post office box. The price is just 60,000 rupiah per year, and it is the best solution for receiving mail, if your post office has one available. The other advantage is there is no interruption to your mail if you move, and the post office will hold your mail if you are away on holidays.

While I have read reports of foreigners having problems with the post in Bali, personally I have never had any trouble and I receive mail and packages fairly regularly from overseas.

If you would like to send small to medium packages overseas, the EMS service is perfect for this. You receive a tracking number, which you can follow the delivery status on the internet. Prices are fairly reasonable and delivery to most overseas destinations is about 5-7 days. You can find more details at their website: ems.posindonesia.co.id

Keeping in touch with friends and family back home

Keeping in touch with friends and family from back home, can help the transition into your new life in Bali and ensure that you don't lose touch with old friends. Thanks to the internet, this is made easier. Skype is the most well known video chat software, but there are several other options also. Apple's Facetime works well between Apple products. Viber enables you to make free international calls using wifi-enabled mobile phones. See their website for more details: www.viber.com

Of course the quality of the service will depend on your internet connection, but I find Telekom Speedy's service to work reasonable enough.

Rubbish Collection (or lack there of)

Perhaps one of the biggest issues facing Bali right now, it the problem of proper waste collection and disposal. Around three quarters of all Bali's rubbish is not collected at all. So what happens to this waste? It is either thrown into forests, rivers, the sea or simply burnt—including plastics, releasing poisonous gases into the air.

There is limited vacant land on the island for landfill. There is however, a growing awareness of the need for recycling. You will often see people collecting plastic drink bottles alongside of the road, which they make a very small amount of money from. Unfortunately, little is done with the rest of the rubbish. While people will collect your garbage, there is a good chance that it will just be taken to a nearby river and dumped.

There are some companies and NGOs that are doing something about the problem. Eco Bali (eco-bali.com) operate a garbage collection service, recycling facilities and they also offer training and education.

Cooking

Balinese living in villages still tend to cook outside, often by burning charcoal, which causes air pollution. The government is subsidizing the cost of gas bottles to improve the air quality, but most families still tend to cook outside. Houses built for westerners will usually come complete with a kitchen (inside the house).

Gas Bottles

There is no piped gas in Bali, so you need to use gas bottles for stoves and sometimes your oven and hot water. The bottles come in two sizes, 15 and 3 kg. Locals are quite deft at carrying a 15kg gas bottle on the back of a motorbike, balancing it with one hand and steering with the other. Some local stores deliver the bottles, along with the gallon drums of water.

Having the gas bottles in or just outside of your house, obviously requires extreme caution. If you do start to smell gas, it usually means the bottle is almost empty. Otherwise the problem could be with the small rubber seal on the gas bottles or with the regulator. It is a good idea to keep a stock of both items, should they need to be replaced.

Many homes will have a cheap two burner stove, called a *gas compo* in Indonesian. These are usually adequate for daily use. A stove/oven combination cooker is a good option if you like baking, or you need more gas burners. Free standing units are ideal if you are renting, as you can easily take it with you, or sell it if you are leaving Bali. UFO (www.ufoelektronika.com) in Denpasar have a good range of kitchen and other electrical appliances.

Learning Bahasa Indonesia

If you want to integrate yourself more into Bali life, learning Indonesian or 'Bahasa Indonesia' is a great way to start. Indonesian people love it when you can speak their language and you will have a much richer experience. Balinese of course have their own language like all ethnic groups across Indonesia. Indonesian is the language which unites the country amongst the diverse ethnic cultures.

Children usually learn Balinese first, and Indonesian later when they attend school. I would suggest learning Indonesian first as you can use it anywhere in Indonesia, and of course there are people from all over the country living in Bali. Indonesian is a relatively easy language to learn, but like any language it is not so easy to master.

Taking classes either at a language school or with a private tutor is a great way to get started.

Here is a list of some of the language schools in Bali:

Indonesia Australia Language Foundation

Australian run program.

Tel: 0361 968 4989

Website: www.ialf.edu

Cinta Bahasa

Based in Ubud, with schools in Canggu and Sanur.

Website: cintabahasa.com

13 GETTING THE RIGHT VISA

Once you have decided you are going to move to Bali, the next step is to work out what visa you are going to apply for. This will of course depend on what you plan to do while you are in Bali, whether you will find a job, start a business, or do volunteer work.

Dealing with immigration in Indonesia is a head ache for most expats. Fortunately, there are a number of companies in Bali that act as agents, who can apply for visas on your behalf. Immigration offices can be a little intimidating for new comers, so you may want to, at least initially, use an agent. Their fees however are expensive, but for many people it is worth the extra money.

Visa on Arrival (VOA)

If you are coming to Indonesia for a holiday, most people will be eligible for a VOA, or Visa on Arrival. The cost is US$25, payable in cash when you arrive at the airport. The visa is good for 30 days (including the day you arrive) and can be extended one time, for a stay of 30 more days. You can extend your visa at any immigration office and you should do it at least 7 days before your current visa expires.

Social Visa

The social visa or Social Budaya visa, is for people coming to

Indonesia to visit family, to take a study course or conduct research. Working on a social visa is prohibited. The visa is good for 60 days (although some embassies may only give you 30 days) and can be extended for a further month, up to four times. So you can have a maximum stay of six months in Indonesia, before having to leave the country.

You need to apply for the social visa outside of Indonesia, at an Indonesian embassy or consulate. You need a sponsor who is an Indonesian citizen, living in Bali. Your sponsor's address on their ID card (KTP) needs to be in Bali. They don't necessarily have to be born there. Your sponsor needs to write a letter saying they will sponsor you, and sign it. You also need a copy of their KTP card and two passport photos (preferably with a red background).

If you are applying at an embassy or consulate other than Singapore or Malaysia, you may need to show a return air ticket. Generally speaking the embassy and consulates in Malaysia and Singapore tend to be the easiest place to apply for the social visa. In Singapore there are even agents who for a fee, apply for the visa on your behalf and you don't even need to step inside the embassy or fill out any forms. At the embassy in Malaysia, you can get the visa in two days. Apply in the morning and then pick it up in the afternoon the next day. In Singapore, using an agent, you can get it in one day.

To renew your visa, you need to visit the immigration office closest to where you are living. You can do it yourself by filling in the forms and submitting them, or an agent can apply on your behalf. If you do it yourself, it generally takes three visits to the immigration office. The first visit to submit the application, the second to pay the fee, and the third to finally pick up your passport. You need to apply for the extension at least 1-2 weeks before your visa is set to expire, so pretty much once you renew your visa, you need start the whole process all over again!

It is not surprising then that many people use an agent for their extensions. Some people even leave their passport with the agent and let them handle every extension. I would advise against doing this, as you are putting a great deal of faith in your agent, as there is always some chance they forget to do an extension. I also like to always have my passport with me.

Business Visa

The business visa as the name suggests, is for people wanting to visit Indonesia to do business. A business visa, however, does not allow you to work. You can use a business visa for example, to research business opportunities or even start a business, but you cannot actually do some kind of job in that business.

You can get a single or multiple entry business visa. The single entry visa is good for 30 days and it can be extended for a further 30 days, two times. If you will be traveling regularly outside of the country, you might consider the multiple entry business visa. The visa is good for 60 days and you can extend it for a further stay of 30 days, four times.

Spouse Visa

If you are married to an Indonesian citizen, you can apply for a spouse visa. The visa is valid for 1 year. After you have renewed the visa two times, you can apply for a five year visa (KITAP). You cannot work on this visa.

Retirement Visa

The retirement visa is for people over 55 years of age, and looking to spend their retirement in Indonesia. You need to have proof of income of more than US$1,500 a month, and employ at least one Indonesian person, to work in your home. For the retirement visa, you have to use the services of a registered agent to get the visa, and they become your sponsor. The cost is about 5-7 million rupiah per year.

Working Visa

To work legally in Indonesia, you need a work permit. Indonesia is very strict about foreigners working illegally and there are hefty fines and the likelihood of immediate deportation if anyone is found to be working illegally.

A work permit is referred to as an "IMTA" or Ijin Mempekerjakan Tenaga Kerja Asing in Indonesian. Only medium to large Indonesian companies can hire foreigners, so you can forget about that cook's job in your local warung. It is also expensive for companies to employ foreigners. Aside from the cost of getting the visa, you need to pay a "training tax" of US$1,200 per year.

Work permits are issued to companies, rather than individuals, so if you quit or lose your job, you also lose your work permit. You also can only work in the role which you got the work permit for.

What is a KITAS exactly?

You often hear people using the acronym "KITAS" when talking about visas in Indonesia. KITAS is an abbreviation of *Kartu Izin Tinggal Terbatas* or Temporary Stay Permit Card. The cards are given for working, spouse, student or retirement visas. It is literally just a card, the size of a business card, and doesn't even come laminated. It is however a very important card, and you shouldn't lose it!

When you get a KITAS, you also get a *Buku Pengawasan Orang Asing*, or *buku POA*. It looks like a passport and it is used to record things like changes in visa status, change of address, birth of children etc. It is a good idea to staple your KITAS card into the book, which helps to keep the documents together.

A KITAS is generally required to open a bank account in Indonesia. It is also compulsory for buying a car or motorbike. Some hospitals, hotels and attractions in Bali give discounts for KITAS holders. Waterbom in Kuta for example gives KITAS holders the same entrance price as locals.

Visa Agents in Singapore

Singapore is the closest flight from Bali, if you need to apply or pick up a visa from outside of the country. It is the only place also that has agents who help you to get the visas. The following agents are widely used by foreigners in Bali.

Ismail Visa Consultant
190 Clemenceau Avenue #02-16
Singapore Shopping Centre
Singapore 239924

Office telephone: (65) 6334 5520
Handphone: 9636 4854
Fax No: (65) 6334 5518

Malik Yusof
Telephone: +65 9675 3307
malksav@hotmail.com

Visa Agents in Bali

I get frequent emails through my website from people asking me about which visa agent I recommend. The problem is that just because one person has a good experience with an agent, someone else could have nothing but problems.

I have heard complaints of pretty much all of the major visa agencies in Bali, which makes me apprehensive about recommending a specific agency. All I can suggest is to pick up the Bali Advertiser and meet with all of the agents, that are located close to where you are living.

You can also ask friends for a recommendation. The important thing is, if you decide to use an agent, try to still find out the basic process yourself. Be careful not to rely on them to remember to process your renewals, as I know of several people who have overstayed their visa because their agent didn't renew their visa.

14 SCAMS AND WARNINGS

When you first move to Bali, you will be eager to make new friends and not upset anyone. This is the time unfortunately that you are the most vulnerable to falling victim to a scam. It pays to be a little cautious of people you meet in the beginning and I am not just talking about locals, as there are a few dubious foreigners also living in Bali, who prey on new arrivals.

Gas scam

Since there is no piped gas in Indonesia, everyone uses gas bottles for cooking and sometimes for hot water. It can be a bit worrying at first, and takes some time to get used to. So the gas scam may touch on this fear.

The scam plays out something like this. Two official looking people will come to your house claiming to be from the government, asking to check the regulators on your gas bottles. They will more than likely carry a clipboard and wear badges to add to their credibility. They proceed to check your gas bottles and then will say there is a problem with your regulator. Of course they conveniently have some available for you to buy, for an overly inflated price. Regulators are inexpensive and available at any hardware store.

We experienced the scam, but I had already read about it on an internet forum. My wife didn't know about it. When I asked the guy to leave, he became pretty angry. It is a good lesson to not let anyone you don't know into your property. If you employ staff, you should instruct your staff to do the same.

Accident/police scam

This scam works on a parent's worst fears, with their child getting into some kind of accident or in trouble with the police. The scammers somehow get your home number and call you stating that your child has been in a serious accident. They claim your child has been taken to hospital and needs some kind of emergency medical need.

You are then asked to transfer money into a bank account, so the hospital can proceed with the treatment. Of course your child is safely at school. There is a similar scam, where the person calling says they are the police and your child has landed in some kind of trouble, drugs for example, with a demand for money to resolve the problem.

John recalls his experience:

> *"It's late on a Sunday night.*
>
> *Around 3.30 am the phone rings.*
>
> *You answer.*
>
> *You hear a young male voice crying and pleading for help.*
>
> *The voice might belong to somebody in your family, but you're not sure yet.*
>
> *Another older voice claims to be police and tells you:*
>
> *"We have just arrested your son in a drug raid with his friends. We can return him to you if you agree to pay us some money. The total will be Rp 50 million for his release. We will need a deposit of Rp 5 million immediately.*
>
> *Because of the seriousness of this offence, if you don't comply we will beat him up and shoot him in the leg. Do not call any other police because what we are offering you is illegal and our commander will be unhappy.*
>
> *If you don't comply, you will not see your son for a very long time."*

What would you do in this situation?

Panic, perhaps? Make your own demands of the "police" (not really an option)? Or pay some money up-front and hope for the best?

This really happened to us a few days ago. We transferred the $500 to some BCA account. Of course, I was getting more suspicious by the moment. However, my wife was extremely distraught (understandably).

Driving back home from the ATM gave us some time to re-evaluate the situation.

Back home, the caller kept phoning and telling us all kinds of nonsense. We asked to talk directly to our son (who doesn't live with us).

They put on some guy who doesn't even speak my wife's native language so the penny (rupiah ?) finally dropped. We were scammed.

To give the scammers some credit, (where credit isn't due), the production was mostly quite well thought out. Background sound effects like a typewriter typing a "report". Various serious-sounding voices sounding busy processing stuff.

I mentioned this story to a medical specialist I am seeing in Denpasar a couple of nights ago and was told of another scam that happened to her.

Phone call. Your child is unconscious. Blah-blah-blah. Being a doctor, she immediately asked for more details that weren't forthcoming.

The calls stopped."

You need to be very careful who you give your telephone number to. Also advise your staff as to whether they can give out your mobile number and in what circumstances. It is common for Indonesian people to ask personal questions, even if you have just met. Be careful about telling people detailed information like where you live or work.

15 THINGS TO DO IN BALI

Since Bali is a popular tourist destination, there are plenty of natural and man made attractions to experience. They make great days out for kids of any ages. With the mostly great year round weather, there are some fantastic outdoor activities and sports for your kids to try. Many of the attractions are a little on the expensive side, but some places offer discounts for KITAS holders and Indonesian citizens. You will need to show your KITAS to get the discount.

This is a sample of some of the places we have enjoyed and is certainly not intended to replace one of the many guidebooks and internet guides to Bali.

Water Bom Bali

There are several water parks in Bali, but Water Bom is hands down the best. The park is set in lush tropical gardens and there are different play areas for all ages. The park is well run and extremely clean. They also have a discount for locals and KITAS holders.

Website: www.waterbom-bali.com

Peek A Boo

Peek A Boo is an air-conditioned indoor playground for kids, conveniently located in Sanur. It is open from 9 am to 6 pm, everyday.

Website: www.peekaboofun.com

Bali Safari and Marine Park

Have a range of animal and educational shows.

Website: www.balisafarimarinepark.com

Bali Bird Park

Large number of species from all over Indonesia and the world. Located close to the Bali Zoo, just out of Ubud.

Website: http://www.bali-bird-park.com/

Bali Zoo

Bali Zoo is a little on the small side, but they still have a good range of animals and the grounds are well maintained. They have a discount for KITAS holders.

Website: www.bali-zoo.com

Bali Elephant Park and Lodge

Operated by Bali Adventure Tours, the Bali Elephant Park and Lodge is an elephant zoo set in a tropical botanical garden.

Website: http://www.baliadventuretours.com/index.php/en/elephant-safari-park/safari-park/about-safari-park

Bali Green Camp

Bali Green Camp is part of the Green School in Ubud and offers a number of different educational programs for kids.

Website: www.greencampbali.com

Other places which have holiday activities include: 3V Kerobokan (http://www.3vkerobokan.com/) and Seminyak Spice (http://seminyakspice.com/services/)

Center Stage

Center Stage is a music and drama school located in Kerobokan.

Website: cmsbali.com

Bali Circus

Bali Circus offers interesting fitness and physical development classes. Kids can learn juggling, hula hoop and trapeze. They have classes for kids aged two and up to adults.

Website: http://balicircus.com/

Canggu Club

Canggu Club is a membership based club offering a range of sporting, restaurant and relaxation facilities. There is an initial membership fee and ongoing fees. You sometimes see 'second-hand' memberships for sale in the Bali Advertiser and on classified websites.

Website: www.cangguclub.com

16 BALI BUSINESS GUIDE

The following are some businesses that I came across while researching this book, which could be of interest to families moving to Bali.

Pro Education

ProEducaiton was started by a former Australian teacher. They provide tutoring and help with students who have special needs.

Website: www.proed.asia

Bali Baby

Bali Baby rents a range of baby gear to save you the trouble of having to bring it from your home country. Bulky items like car seats and cots can be rented through Bali Baby. The business is aimed more at short term tourists as if you are staying long term in Bali, it would probably work out cheaper buying or bringing your own supplies.

Website: balibaby.com

Bali Pool Fence Hire

Gates and fences around pools are very rare in Bali and is a potential nightmare for any parent. Bali Pool Fence Hire offers an innovative solution, bamboo fencing which can installed around most pools and is ideal for people renting a villa.

Check out their website for more details and contact information: balipoolfencehire.com

Bali Babysitting Service

Australian operated and managed baby sitting and nanny service: www.balisbestbabysitting.com

Bali Insect Screens

Most houses and villas don't have fly screens and they are not easily available. Bali Insect Screens has an easy to install system using a 3M product.

Web: www.baliinsectscreens.com

17 INTERNET RESOURCES

Facebook has many Bali expat related groups, with new ones being started everyday. Here is a list of the more active groups. If you prefer a more traditional forum, check out the Bali expat forum (http://balipod.com/).

Facebook Groups

Bali Expats: https://www.facebook.com/groups/100931413283083/

Bali Babies: https://www.facebook.com/groups/balibabies/

Green School Parents:
https://www.facebook.com/groups/greenschoolparents/

Bali House and Accommodation:
https://www.facebook.com/groups/231171780241689/

Bali House and Accommodation (for properties in the south of Bali)
https://www.facebook.com/groups/148203102026630/

Bali Buy and Sell (for second-hand goods)
https://www.facebook.com/groups/148203102026630/

Ubud Community:

https://www.facebook.com/groups/149393691784641/

Bali Community: https://www.facebook.com/groups/balicommunity/

Bali Home Schooling:
https://www.facebook.com/groups/121606311286466/

Bali Trade's People:
https://www.facebook.com/groups/510832578939216/

18 EXPAT INTERVIEW

Michelle shares her experiences moving to Bali:

How long did it take for your kids to adjust to living in Bali?

We have been traveling to Bali for many years and my kids had been here on holidays about four times before we moved here. There are parts of living here that they adjusted to very quickly, I have one child 7 years old who loves living here and another 9 years old, who is maybe just coming to terms with living here after 18months, but who would return to Perth in an instance given the chance, even if that means living with his grandmother and not us his mum, dad and brother.

How did you decide on a school to send your kids?

I had found a small independent international school on the internet before we moved the kids here. We went and saw the school and got the kids to do a few days there while we were on holidays. I chose the school not for the academics but for the environment it said it offered, and also cost was an issue. Schooling in Bali is very expensive and apart from housing, the other biggest expense of living in Bali. We didn't get into this school due to wait lists, the next school we chose was due to it's technology and standard of schooling it offered.

What has been your overall experience with schools in Bali?

Our children have gone to two schools here in Bali, the first was an Australian International School which offers pre-kindy through to year 12. The school was very expensive, but had: small class sizes, Australian teachers, Indonesian assistant teachers and academically was a very good school with high standards. Our children improved and thrived with the smaller class sizes which allowed a lot more one on one time with the teacher. Sadly, we couldn't keep up with the annual rising fees $20,000+ USD for two children.

The other school they are now attending, the small independent school, offers a lovely feel of community and reminds us of what school was like when were children, at half the cost of the other school. It doesn't offer as much, but I don't think school is necessarily all about academics. We are happy here and the kids have made new friends which is lovely.

People must understand when they come to Bali, that schooling is expensive without great facilities, but it is the wonderful multicultural experience the children get and I love that the teachers can give your kids a hug if they need one. Balinese people are caring and love children, I think western countries have made school too formal with ridiculous rules and regulations forgetting kids need to be kids and need more than just academics. Dealing with such multiculturalism here makes for much more flexibility.

What advice would you give to parents for deciding on a school?

Think about what will best suit your kids integration into moving countries, what are you looking for in a school - academics, community, price (can you continue paying the cost of schooling at the school you chose?) , country's curriculum taught at school (in case you are thinking of moving back to your home country in the future). Schooling is also about the parents—it's a great way to meet new people, when shifting to a new country not knowing anyone.

Health is a big concern for many families moving to Bali, what has been your experience and how have you found the level of health care in Bali?

Our main reason for moving to Bali was for health reasons and I have been involved with the hospitals in Bali, both as a tourist and as an expat living here. My youngest son has many health issues, he suffers asthma/dermatitis/croup/anaphylaxis from all nuts/citrus pip's/environmental allergies/staph and suffered a number of chest infections.

We noticed when coming to Bali on holidays, his skin would clear up and when that cleared up this other issues would come under control. Bali doesn't have many pollens like Australia, so for those with allergies it can be a great place to live. We have noticed he now has a lot less frequent asthma attacks, but when he does have them they are a lot worse. He has reduced his medications from 5 - 6 steroids a day to 2 and has gone from daily 48 hour doses of antihistamine to only needing it once a week, or every few weeks.

I also have a few heart conditions, and moving here allowed us to have help around the house and be less stressed/rushed. It was another reason for moving here. I have found my heart condition to be much better controlled and I feel much healthier. Before moving here I contacted the one international hospital I knew of, to find out the types of specialists they had, and the procedures they could offer relating to our personal needs.

Once living here and knowing more about the island there are several hospitals to chose from and many specialists, however, not all that you may need. It is also important to come with detailed information on any health care issues you have, call the hospitals, find out what they offer and find a specialist that you are comfortable with, who understands your conditions and can manage them.

We needed a paediatrician, I found one at the new hospital here Siloam (definitely my choice of hospital) I met with her, went through all my sons medical issues, spoke about medications and checked that she knew/understood everything. Thankfully our experience was good, we found a very good English speaking doctor, who knew everything we needed, understood the medications and importantly, was easy to have a relationship with. Doctors here give out their personal mobile numbers and it is fine to contact them directly. This I love and feel very reassured about.

Unfortunately most of the medications needed for both my son and myself are not sold in Bali. All of ours are bought in Australia and we do a big medications run twice a year, which I pay full price for in Australia.

When traveling with medications, have notes from your doctor, so they can easily be brought into Bali. Even in international hospitals, you find things are more relaxed. Sometimes it can be hard to get clear information from reception/nurses, but generally speaking, once dealing with the doctor, they are very helpful and speak good English (in international hospitals).

Ask for prices before seeing the doctor, or any procedures are carried out. Also, doctors often give a lot of medication here when sick, the usual is three lots. It was strange to get used to at first. I have also been to the local hospital as a tourist, and I have to say, it was a scary experience and not one I would want to have again. In the emergency department, there are no sheets on the bed, no curtains/privacy between the beds, no medication (so pain relief) is given without first paying for it and many locals can't afford it.

Any and all family can come in. I was fortunate to get the one and only doctor who spoke English. There was mold on the walls/ceiling and I left with a broken elbow, but was told it was badly bruised. I would definitely spend the extra money and go to an international hospital. Also, it is great to have good equipment here, but along with that equipment make sure there are doctors and nurses, who know how to use it and can diagnose you. Finally, you need an action plan for getting to the hospital if you are really sick, while there are ambulances here, traffic is such an issue and waiting for an ambulance to come to you, and then go to hospital, is unrealistic time wise.

Did you hire a nanny/maid and how did you go about finding someone?

We have had a few different nanny/maids since living here. Some were provided with the villa we rented, and some were through just asking local people if they knew anyone, or asking other expats to ask their staff if they knew someone.

There are agencies you can use here. Make sure you are specific with what you want them to do— teach them, watch them, and remember they can only do what you show them. Treat them with kindness and they will generally be good to you.

Is there anything you would recommend people bringing from home that you can not find in Bali?

As mentioned before, definitely check if your specific medications are sold or ordered in Bali. Never let them run down low as nothing works fast in Bali. If they can be ordered, it could be many weeks before they come, if they even do come.

Food is something we miss a lot from home, we regularly ask friends visiting to bring things for us. Hair care products is another thing we bring (waxes, hairspray etc not shampoo). Also while you can get them, things like cards, wrapping paper etc I bring from home, as you can't just go to the shop and get them easily, as I found out the first time I needed kids birthday cards— on the party day!

What are some activities your kids enjoy in Bali?

Since moving here as an expat, we have realised there are many kids activities that most tourists do not even know about. Our kids did a Lego based Robotics course, which actually has Olympic competitions within Indonesia. This is good for both boys and girls— drum lessons, music production courses, horse riding, many fun parks, all kinds of sports, handicraft, jet skiing, banana boat riding and body surfing. You name it, it's here and more!

Finally what advice would you give to anyone considering moving to Bali with their kids?

Before deciding where you will live chose a school, then the location you will live. You don't want to be stuck in traffic for hours going to and from school and after school activities. Let your kids try some schools, while you are here on holidays.

Make sure you are a hands on parent—don't leave your children to be raised by the people who work for you. Know your kids and what's going on in their life.

It is a big move shifting countries. Personally, I think moving for just one year, is a big upheaval for your kids. Decide is this where you really want your future to be, make sure you have patience and flexibility. Knowing the language is a huge bonus and helpful to learn when you get here.

19 FINAL THOUGHTS

There have been many news stories, mostly in the Australian media about families, who have moved to Bali. Almost every article has focused a great deal on the positives of moving. In this book, I have tried to point out some of the difficulties of living in Bali, so you can be at least a little bit prepared, if you decided to go ahead with the move.

As Patricia, the Green School parent said, "Don't be seduced by the hype of having your kids in Green School before finding out whether it will suit your kid and your family." I think this can be said equally of moving to Bali.

There are some people who strongly question families that bring their kids to Bali, mainly because of a perceived lower standard of education. I think I was even in denial about the schools, until I started researching them more. It did make me start to wonder whether I was putting my own interests ahead of my own child's future.

I do feel however, that families who move from a western country to Bali, are looking something different not only for themselves, but their children also. I think they believe they will experience something different in Bali, that will be of future benefit for their family, and will be better than what they might be miss out on in a formal education.

I hope that you can now make a better informed decision about moving to Bali and this guide has been helpful to at least ease the transition. I do enjoy helping people and if you have any further questions about life in Bali, please do not hesitate to email me at: mike@baliexpat.com

You can also reach me on Facebook: http://www.facebook.com/baliexpats and Twitter: @baliexpat

Printed in Great Britain
by Amazon.co.uk, Ltd.,
Marston Gate.